Create a Christ-centered home by teaching spiritual lessons as part of your family's everyday life. Filled with object lessons, practical tips, and ideas for creating teaching moments, this book will build testimonies and family relationships in a natural, authentic way.

Learn to

- Increase the quality and quantity of teaching moments
- Teach about the Holy Ghost with object lessons
- Enhance family scripture study and family home evening
- Focus on the small and simple joys of life that so often get overlooked
- See the importance of parenting with an eternal perspective

Perfect for parents, Primary teachers, and youth leaders, this book not only teaches you what to teach, but also *how* to teach, so you can share memorable moments with the children you love and instill valuable lessons that will last their whole lives.

{
"*Table Salt & Testimony* is an instruction manual designed for the family classroom—where the most important educators in the Church teach the children of Zion every day."

—Stephen J. Stirling, author of *Shedding Light on the Dark Side* and *Persona Non Grata*
}

SCAN to visit

ALSO AVAILABLE AS AN
EBOOK

CFI
CEDAR FORT
Publishing & Media
AN IMPRINT OF CEDAR FORT, INC.

ISBN 978-1-4621-1627-0   USA $11.99 C/

9 781462 116270
51

WWW.DARRENESCHMIDT.COM

WWW.CEDARFORT.COM

Praise for

Table Salt & Testimony

"A must read! I loved this book and was able to take out several concrete suggestions that will bless my family and me. I have admired the Schmidt family for many years and am glad that Darren is now sharing some of the secrets of their success. Practical and inspiring!"

—John Hilton III, religious educator and author of *The Little Book of Book of Mormon Evidences*, *52 Life Changing Questions*, and *Why?*

"There is no more critical need in Zion than for parents who understand their sacred roles as teachers of the gospel in the home. Darren Schmidt's *Table Salt and Testimony* meets that need with real-world perspectives in parenting from the scriptures and from words of the modern prophets, along with practical applications gleaned from the experience of a master teacher. *Table Salt and Testimony* is an instruction manual designed for the family classroom—where the most important educators in the Church teach the children of Zion every day."

—Stephen J. Stirling, author of *Shedding Light on the Dark Side* and *Persona Non Grata*

"I loved *Table Salt and Testimony*! I've worked with elite organizations and teams where the stakes are high and optimal performance is a must. However, no team is more important than the family. The role parents play in effectively teaching their children in the home is paramount. Through the use of effective storytelling and simple how-to strategies, Darren Schmidt does a great job in helping us know how to teach our children so gospel learning can go from their heads down into their hearts."

—Justin Su'a, mental conditioning coach and author of *Parent Pep Talks* and *Mentally Tough Teens*

TABLE

Salt &

TESTIMONY

TABLE Salt & TESTIMONY

{ IDEAS, OBJECT LESSONS & PRACTICAL
PARENTING TIPS FOR CREATING
TEACHING MOMENTS IN THE HOME }

DARREN E. SCHMIDT

CFI
An Imprint of Cedar Fort, Inc.
Springville, Utah

ISBN 13: 978-1-4621-1627-0

Published by CFI, an imprint of Cedar Fort, Inc.
2373 W. 700 S., Springville, UT 84663
Distributed by Cedar Fort, Inc., www.cedarfort.com

LIBRARY OF CONGRESS CATALOGING-IN-PUBLICATION DATA

Schmidt, Darren E., 1976- author.
Table salt and testimony / Darren E. Schmidt.
    pages cm
Includes bibliographical references.
ISBN 978-1-4621-1627-0 (alk. paper)
1. Families--Religious life. 2. Parenting--Religious aspects--Church of Jesus Christ of Latter-day Saints. 3. Church of Jesus Christ of Latter-day Saints--Doctrines. 4. Mormon Church--Doctrines. I. Title.

BX8643.F3S36 2015
248.8'450882893--dc23

2015001342

Cover design by Shawnda T. Craig
Cover design © 2015 Lyle Mortimer
Edited and typeset by Jessica B. Ellingson

Printed in Canada

10 9 8 7 6 5 4 3 2 1

Printed on acid-free paper

For all those who seek to improve.

Contents

Foreword

In our home, we have always enjoyed the Olympics and watched them faithfully and consistently hoping to see a great "Olympic moment," where dreams become reality and the unexpected sometimes takes center stage over the expected. One such moment occurred during the figure skating final of the 2002 Olympics in Salt Lake City, Utah. Our family sat around the television and watched with excitement while a young woman from America who was previously picked to place fifth by the experts unexpectedly won the gold medal after a nearly flawless performance. Loud cheers filled our home as we watched with great anticipation as this "dream come true" moment was caught on film. As we watched, however, I couldn't help but notice that the cameraman was purposely spending at least twice as much of the camera time catching the many expressions of the mother, who was anxiously jumping up and down in total elation, and not the daughter who had actually won the gold medal! Tears of joy ran down the mother's cheeks as she both laughed and cried. For a moment, it was as if the whole world stood still out of reverence for such a priceless and sacred parental moment.

I realized then that the cameraman knew exactly what he was doing, as did the rest of the broadcasters and media personnel. Later, while I contemplated the special joy I saw on the mother's face and considered my own special parenting moments, into my mind came the oft-quoted words, "For behold, this is *my work and my glory*—to bring to pass the immortality and eternal life of man" (Moses 1:39; italics added). Surely our Father in Heaven is stating His very purpose and work in this verse: exalting His children with the priceless gift of immortality and eternal life. But I also believe that He—our perfect, immortal, omnipotent, and Eternal Father—is expressing His inner joy and the personal excitement He feels as He enjoys each and every moment of our personal journey toward godhood with us, it being His "glory." Think of the great moments you have had as a parent. Wouldn't you agree that seeing your child improve or accomplish something great far outweighs many of the other joys that you have experienced in this life, including your own successes or personal achievements? Would you also agree that, like Heavenly Father, inexpressible joy has come to you in this life when you have seen in your own children the reflection of the Savior as they have walked toward His light, followed His example, and gained testimonies for themselves through their own diligence and obedience? In the New Testament, the Apostle John expressed this very sentiment when he said, "I have no greater joy than to hear that my children *walk in truth*" (3 John 1:4; italics added). Sadly, I believe that there are many who have not yet felt or have only partially experienced the joy John is speaking about. I have found through careful study, pondering, and my personal efforts to improve as a parent that not only is this joy made available to all who are humble seekers of the truth, but it is the essence of why we are here on earth: that we might have joy in our families and our posterity. In this book, I have sought to present some principles of parenting, along with various ideas and suggestions to apply those principles in the home, in the hopes that your children may more often be found walking in the truth. Most of what I will share and seek to express in this book has come as I have searched for, pondered on, and wrestled with how to implement in my family and home the direction that has been given in the scriptures from a loving Father in Heaven as well as the words of modern and living prophets. What began with a small file entitled "Dad—How can I be a better?" has grown as I have sought to improve, discover, and apply the things I have found from these reliable sources. It is my hope in this book to share with you some of those discoveries, reflections, considerations, ponderings, and personal experiences I have had along the way, both good and bad. I hope that in the process of reading this book, you may have your own reflections and impressions specific to your own circumstances and needs.

Acknowledgments

I am personally and profoundly grateful to all those who have contributed to this book, including family, friends, and colleagues, with suggestions, direction, help, personal insights, and editing. I have in no way done this on my own. I have been taught by so many remarkable people and parents through their words, lives, and examples, including my own parents, James and Susan Schmidt; and my brother, Brent, and sisters, Amy, Andrea, Annette, and Ashley, who have blessed me in so many ways. I want to thank my sweetheart, Jolynn, the love of my life, who has been with me every step of the way, encouraging me, teaching me, and loving me all these years. I am also grateful beyond words for each of my precious children, who have helped to teach me many of the truths I will discuss in this book and brought more joy into my life than I ever thought possible! Thank you Patrick, Maylin, Cameron, Sydney, Celeste, Joshua, Michael, and Christian! I love each of you! Most important, I want to thank my Heavenly Father, who has blessed me with so much and has been so patient with me as I have sought to improve myself and become more like Him with the help of His Son, Jesus Christ, whom I also love and honor. I hope this book can in some way help express

Darren E. Schmidt

the gratitude and deep love I feel for Them and for the understanding They have given me over the years through the aid of the Holy Spirit.

CHAPTER 1

"So I'm a Parent. Now What?"

I awoke suddenly in panic during the earliest hours of the morning to the sounds of a wife in unbearable pain. My sweetheart, though handling the labor pains well, had certainly made it clear that she was uncomfortable and wanted her suffering quickly resolved. After almost thirty hours of labor pains for her, me trying to give what little physical and emotional comfort I could, and more challenges than I ever want to remember or write about, the time for the birth of our first child was close at hand! As the grand conclusion drew closer, I remember thinking that I was far too tired to appreciate anything and wondered if I could handle, or even really wanted, the responsibilities or sacred trust of being a parent. Then suddenly, the wonderful moment arrived, a most priceless and precious moment when heaven certainly touched the earth, bringing to it an eternal treasure. Realizing there was no way back now, I really had no other choice than to press forward in faith, hoping I had what it took to be a good parent and that there would be moments of joy along the way that would make it all worth it. It didn't take more than a couple days after bringing our little one home before the reality of being a parent started to set in. A few baby cards I read helped to express some of my inner feelings:

- Congratulations! . . . on moving out of labor and into management.
- I wish babies were more like remote controls with on-off switches and volume-control buttons.
- Congratulations on your new arrival! Enjoy the diapers and vomit!
- *Baby. Niño. Le bebe. Bambino. Papoose.* It all means the same thing: no sleep for the big people!
- Congratulations! You'll never sleep again!

Having now gone through this same difficult and wonderful process eight times and being incredibly blessed with five boys and three girls, my wife and I can honestly say that we understand a little more what it truly means to be exhausted and overwhelmed.

{ Change Your Mindset }

When the chuckles from the baby cards fade and the smoke finally clears after the nine months of anticipating your new arrival, what comes next? President David O. McKay once stated that of all the effective places in the world for children to learn the lessons of life, the home was the "most effective place." He said that "nothing can take the place of home in rearing and teaching children" and that whatever successes a parent might achieve outside of the home would never successfully "compensate for failure in the home."[1] Be honest now. Have you ever been guilty of thinking or believing that a Primary teacher, seminary teacher, or Young Men or Young Women leader is more effective at teaching your children the lessons of life, as President McKay called them, than you are? Have you ever been guilty of thinking that your talents and abilities could be put to better use elsewhere than in your home?

Consider for a moment a father who prepares a marvelous presentation at work to the praise and applause of everyone in the office and then comes home Monday evening and throws something together for his family night at the last minute, giving a mediocre effort at best, with little thought of what he is teaching or what the needs of the family are. Think of the praise and attention a mother might

2

receive when she faithfully serves in the Relief Society presidency, spending a great deal of time out doing good, but then neglects precious teaching moments with her children because she claims she is too tired or too busy from the day's activities to give them nurture, love, or instruction. I certainly don't want to downplay the need or importance of callings and responsibilities in the Church or the need for good and effective leaders and teachers who impact the lives of the youth in a profound way. But if we expect those leaders and teachers to be doing the things we should be doing and will be the most effective at doing according to prophets, then perhaps we are saying through our thoughts or our actions that we really don't believe the home is the most effective place for the rearing and spiritual development of our children. Elder David A. Bednar once said that he would not "trust [his] children exclusively to the programs of the Church" and that "the Church operates as a support . . . as we create a home that is a house of learning." He said that it is the responsibility of us as parents to "create a Christ-centered, Spirit-filled home environment where the Holy Ghost can teach and testify to our children."[2] This is certainly easier said than done, but I have found that parenting that makes a difference starts with our beliefs and getting our heads and hearts wrapped around the idea that, as President Harold B. Lee once said, the most important work we will do will take place "within the walls of [our] own homes."[3]

{ We Learn by Doing }

In Doctrine and Covenants 2, we learn that power and authority were given directly from John the Baptist to Joseph Smith and Oliver Cowdery, along with the instruction to baptize one another. I imagine that during this process, John the Baptist must have offered some direction on how to baptize, the words to say, and how and where to place one's hands for convenience during the baptism process. He must have also (having himself baptized multitudes of people before) instructed Joseph and Oliver about the importance of making sure the baptismal recipient was fully and completely immersed in the water. I cannot help but wonder why John did not baptize Joseph and Oliver himself. He certainly had the authority and the ability to do so, having proven it by giving them the Aaronic Priesthood by the laying on of hands.

Think of how incredible it might have been for Joseph and Oliver to report that they had been baptized by he who baptized the Savior Himself, John the Baptist, a resurrected being. Yet the Lord saw wisdom in letting Joseph and Oliver do the baptizing themselves with perhaps the understanding that both Joseph and Oliver would need this experience later. Heavenly Father could have easily built the ark for the prophet Noah or made the plates for Nephi. He could have built the Kirtland Temple for the Saints, who were poor, impoverished, and severely persecuted in the process of building it. Yet He allowed and encouraged these men and women to do things that would help them to grow as individuals and develop godlike traits necessary for eternity and, more specifically, eternal life with their Father in Heaven. Surely our Father in Heaven could do a much better job of parenting our children than we could. Yet He places that child, His child, into our arms along with His sacred trust and encouraging love, expecting and knowing we have the potential to accomplish great things and that He can give us assistance when the need arises and we seek His help. "Please take care of my little one," I can almost hear Him say while passing that precious child from His perfect hands into our earthly fallen ones.

{ Focus on Progressing Instead of Perfection }

Our responsibilities to take care of, teach, love, nurture, and build our Father in Heaven's children can be intimidating and certainly overwhelming as we learn by *doing*. But I have taken courage from this statement made by President Howard W. Hunter: "The direction we are moving is more important than a particular degree of perfection."[4] All too often we might measure our parenting in terms of how other parents around us are doing or according to an unattainable expectation about what the perfect parent should be, focusing more on what we lack than where we are going. If we will instead look to improve our efforts over time by making small and gradual changes consistently, then I believe we will find less frustration in our parenting and more fruit. Nephi, the Book of Mormon prophet, had to go to the mount "oft" before he was able to build the ship "after the manner [of] the Lord," and upon the ship's completion, his brethren marveled (1 Nephi 18:2–4). We too must work at our parenting, praying often about it, taking frequent trips to the mountains (the temple), and making the needed adaptations to our growing families in patience and in faith if we are to ever build a family worthy of marveling and eventually arrive at the "promised land" (see 1 Nephi 17–18).

You will remember that instead of fully engaging in the tasks before them, Laman and Lemuel spent their time looking at what they left behind (Jerusalem). Later, they became content with their lives by the seashore, wondering if the promised land was really better and worth the sacrifices they had made to obtain it. We must be cautious that this belief or attitude does not find its way into our own hearts. As parents, we must remember that a successful harvest does not come in the fall without diligent planting and consistent nourishment of the garden in the spring. In the book of Galatians, Paul reminds us, "Be not deceived; God is not mocked: for whatsoever a man soweth, that shall he also reap. . . . And let us not be weary in well doing: for in due season we shall reap, if we faint not" (Galatians 6:7, 9).

To further illustrate this principle, I want to share a tragic story of a friend and neighbor we have gotten to know and love over the years. Once, during a friendly visit with this elderly woman at her home, she confided in me (I'm sure she was trying to teach a young father something) that years earlier, she had diligently prepared and presented lessons for family home evening. But her husband had been critical of her teaching methods and abilities, even while she was teaching the children, expecting more or "perfection." He criticized and yet offered no help or positive encouragement, which made doing it all the more difficult. She worked hard at it weekly, but as the months passed, she could no longer bear his demeaning remarks and criticism. Finally, she gave up the fight, and family home evenings—as well as family scripture studies—were abandoned altogether. I saw in her eyes much regret as she shared this with me. She then spoke with great sadness about the inactivity of the majority of her children in the Church and their disobedience to its teachings.

This she believed had occurred in part because of her decision years earlier to abandon all family instruction.

Interestingly enough, her husband was still living at the time she shared this with me. He was not living with her and hadn't for a few years due to several health problems that required him to be taken care of at a special care facility. Later, as a member of the bishopric, I visited this man in the facility and witnessed tears roll down his cheeks as he expressed, as best as he could, the desire he had to be forgiven of his past wrongs, including those toward his family. He did not disclose the past wrongs toward his family, but I knew them, at least in part, because of the discussion I had previously had with his wife. What a tragic story of regret this is! Surely no family is too far removed from the outstretched hands of a loving Savior, who can heal emotional, mental, and physical pain and restore love and peace to a family through humility and forgiveness. I think He has healed and restored to some measure in this family, but think of the suffering and pain that could have been avoided had both these parents been focusing on improving (the process) and not on being perfect (the product). None of us will teach perfect lessons. None of us will hold perfect family scripture studies or always say the right things at the right times to our children, but we should always be striving to do the very best we can, seeking always to improve while never being too hard on ourselves. We should know that our complete efforts, though perhaps only a few meager loaves and fishes, when touched by the Savior can bless, feed, and do more over time than we thought possible.

{ Avoid Comparisons }

Elder Jeffrey R. Holland has said comparing ourselves to others can be destructive and that "no one of us is less treasured or cherished of God than another." He stated that "He [Heavenly Father] loves each of us—insecurities, anxieties, self-image, and all. He doesn't measure our talents or our looks; He doesn't measure our professions or our possessions."[5] And I would add that He doesn't measure our parenting abilities. Whenever I am tempted to compare my own parenting to or judge by others' parenting successes (or failures for that matter), I try to remind myself of the destructive nature of making such comparisons.

Elder Neal A. Maxwell was once heard to say that our loving Father, just as He took the time to place the star in the precise orbit millennia before it was seen over Bethlehem during the birth of the baby Jesus, has "at least" given equal attention to each of us in our own and precise human orbits so that we might give both light and warmth to others as well as receive light and warmth from them.[6] Both of these expressions from apostles deserve our thoughtful consideration and may again require a change in our mindsets and thinking, recognizing that He who knoweth all things has placed each of us in an orbit with parents, siblings, wards, schools, and community associations where we have the best chance for growth, progress, and ultimately eternal life with Him. This might require more faith on the part of those of us who have been born and raised in difficult circumstances, but what it should also do is give us confidence that the Lord trusts us and that we are the best He has to offer (think of the numbers that Father in Heaven had to choose from) for our particular children. If this is the case, then why would we compare ourselves to others when there simply is no comparison! We can have full confidence that our Father in Heaven has chosen each of us individually and specifically as parents, despite our own weaknesses and deficiencies, because He sees something of greatness and eternal significance in what we will do as parents, though we may not see it in ourselves.

King Benjamin, the Nephite prophet and king, reminded us, "Believe in God; believe that he is, and that he created all things, both in heaven and in earth; believe that he has all wisdom, and all power, both in heaven and in earth; believe that man doth not comprehend all the things which the Lord can comprehend" (Mosiah 4:9). May we continue to be reminded of the incredible trust and responsibility that our Father in Heaven has placed upon each of us who parent as well as our dependence on Him in our parenting efforts. Let us be willing to change, if we need to, our thinking and our actions so they match the parenting truths and principles that have been revealed by the Lord. Let us be more effective instruments in God's hands, even the best instruments He has to offer. Let us know that perfection is not something we must achieve in a day, month, year, or even lifetime. It is through the processes of growth, refinement, and improvement that perfection is ultimately achieved.

{ Notes }

1. David O. McKay, *Family Home Evening Manual 1968–69*, iii.
2. David A. Bednar, "Teach Them to Understand," Ricks College Campus Education Week Devotional, June 4, 1998.
3. Harold B. Lee, *Teachings of Presidents of the Church: Harold B. Lee* (Salt Lake City: The Church of Jesus Christ of Latter-Day Saints, 2000), 134.
4. Howard W. Hunter, "The Dauntless Spirit of Resolution," in *Brigham Young University Speeches*, January 5, 1992.
5. Jeffrey R. Holland, "The Other Prodigal," *Ensign*, May 2002.
6. Neal A. Maxwell, *That my Family Should Partake* (Salt Lake City: Deseret Book), 1974.

"By Small and Simple Things"

Years ago, a faithful missionary from Australia who was assigned to my same mission in New Zealand shared with me his remarkable conversion story. After refusing to let the two missionaries into his home, he finally accepted a copy of the Book of Mormon, "just to get rid of them." The book sat for several days before the missionaries returned to see how his reading was going. To their inquiries, he reported that he had not read the book but would try to, if he found the time. Again, it was "just to get rid of them."

Several days passed until one day he found himself flipping through the book curiously "just to look at the pictures." While doing so, a particular picture caught his eye and filled his heart with wonder and amazement. (Those of you familiar with the paperback version of the Book of Mormon will remember that there are pictures contained in its pages, illustrated by the artist Friberg.) The particular picture he gazed at featured the pompous and wicked King Noah on his large golden throne with his appointed wicked priests sitting in judgment, as well as two pet cheetahs sitting close by. Also in the picture, an elderly man, Abinadi, stood in chains in the center of the room. He was delivering a message from heaven and was filled, it appeared, with power and light, having a most radiant countenance.

My missionary friend said that he was so intrigued by the picture that he began searching for the story in the book. As he read, he was filled with the Spirit, knowing that both the story and the words spoken by the prophet Abinadi were true. A short time later, he was taught the gospel in its fulness by the full-time missionaries, and soon after, he was baptized a member of the Church, being the only one in his family to do so. A year later, he put in his papers to serve a full-time mission and teach the things he had been so affected and influenced by. Having known him, I must say that he was as diligent and faithful as any missionary I knew or have ever known. He, like Abinadi, became an instrument in God's hands, standing as a witness "of God at all times and in all things, and in all places" (Mosiah 18:9).

As I have reflected on the Book of Mormon story of Abinadi and King Noah, I have found it remarkable that Alma was the only person, at first glance, who was influenced by Abinadi's message. After fleeing from King Noah's priests, Alma went into hiding and sincerely repented, seeking forgiveness from the Lord. He then wrote out Abinadi's delivered message before beginning to deliver the same message himself. As the story continues, multitudes join Alma at the waters of Mormon also seeking forgiveness and the opportunity to make covenants before the Lord by taking His name upon them and being willing to "mourn with those that mourn" and "comfort those that stand in need of comfort" (ibid.; see Mosiah 12–18). We are told that four hundred and fifty individuals were willing to make these covenants, probably in large part because of Alma's teachings and leadership, which were influenced by the prophet Abinadi's words, testimony, and example of courage and strength (Mosiah 18:35). Thanks to Abinadi planting the right seed at the right time and in the right place through his obedience to the Lord's direction, even under the most trying circumstances, multitudes were blessed, including my missionary friend. He read the story and was influenced by it over two thousand years after it was written, and I'm sure it's the same for countless others!

We must have faith that our diligence and perseverance as parents can and will, like Abinadi, affect future generations. Our direction, love, and teachings must be delivered at all costs. We, like Abinadi, might not witness in this life the full fruits of our labors or understand the full extent of our influence, testimony, teachings, and lessons upon our families. But we can know that our best efforts are pleasing to the Lord and that all we do will eventually bear fruit as we act in faith. We would then see, for example, the extra time we spend preparing a lesson on the Savior for family night as an important use of time, or the few extra moments we spend during a car ride discussing with our children their day's activities as both sacred and necessary, knowing that it is the day-to-day moments that make up eternity. The prophet Alma came to understand this principle well and later taught, after his own change of heart, that "by small and simple things are great things are brought to pass. . . . And the Lord God doth work by means to bring about his great and eternal purposes" (Alma 37:6–7). If our Father in Heaven works by small means to achieve His purposes and has proven this time and time again, then we should expect that our successes and progression as parents should come through similarly small means.

President Boyd K. Packer, current President of the Quorum of the Twelve Apostles, has been a great example to me of this principle. A few years ago, I was impressed by his collection of carved birds, paintings of nature, and artwork that was, at that time, on display at the Church History Library in downtown Salt Lake City. Many of the glass bird carvings were so lifelike that I had to stop my small children from tapping on the glass; they were so sure that the birds they saw were real. The entire room was full of some of the most incredible artwork and carvings I have ever seen, and all of it bore the same name: Boyd K. Packer.

Having read much on President Packer, including his biography (I've always loved and admired him), I knew that he had supervised the seminary programs of the Church for many years, traveling, training, and instructing in the seminaries, as well as held some time-consuming Church callings. I knew that he had written a book on teaching, completed a doctorate degree, and—even more remarkable—raised ten children! While I stared at this entire room of artwork, I found myself wondering where he possibly found the time to do it all! As I pondered, I remembered reading that he had set a goal for himself to spend ten quality minutes of his time each day with each of his ten children. He would then take a few minutes, generally in the later evening, when things quieted down to do some of the things he loved, including artwork, drawings, and carvings. He would use this time to unwind and would sometimes even work on his general conference talks. As I considered these things I had read, a sweet feeling came over me. Not only did President Packer have a room full of some of the most amazing creations I have ever seen, but somewhere in the Church, there was a posterity even more magnificent because President Packer had taken the time amidst his busy schedule to be a father. Truly by small and simple things are great things brought to pass.

In stark contrast, I now cite a story that you may be familiar with from Church history, taken from the life of Thomas B. Marsh, who, like President Packer, also served as President of the Quorum of the Twelve Apostles. President Gordon B. Hinckley at general conference told about Brother Marsh's departure from the Church by saying, "He lost his standing in the Church. He lost his testimony of the gospel. For nineteen years he walked in poverty and darkness and bitterness, experiencing illness, and loneliness. He grew old before his time. Finally, like the prodigal son in the parable of the Savior, he recognized his foolishness and painfully made his way to this valley, and asked Brigham Young to forgive him and permit his rebaptism." As the first President of the Council of the Twelve, Brother Marsh had been loved, respected, and honored in the early days of the Church. But he now "asked only that he might be ordained a deacon and become a doorkeeper in the house of the Lord."[1] As the story goes, Brother Marsh died in full fellowship in the Church, but his family never came west as he had to be reunited with the Saints and partake of the full blessings of the gospel. A man I know met an elderly lady several years ago in the Church History Library who was a descendant of Thomas B. Marsh. She claimed that there were over ten thousand descendants of Brother Marsh today (she collected names and worked on the history herself). She also claimed that to her knowledge, *not one* of Brother Marsh's posterity, including her, was currently a member of the Church! How unbelievably tragic this story is! I can't help but wonder how the posterity of Brother Marsh would be different today had he led a life of continued faithfulness and helped his children do the same. Like Brother Marsh, each of us will be put to the test, and generations will be influenced by our parenting decisions. May we never forget the Lord's charge to "lay up for [ourselves] treasures in heaven, where neither moth nor rust doth corrupt, and where thieves do not break through nor steal" (Matthew 6:20). Let us continue to reflect that the earth we stand on would be utterly wasted at the Lord's Coming without forever families sealed in holy temples (see D&C 2). May each of us, like Abinadi, do the things asked of us by the Lord and, in the process, look into the eyes of our children to catch a small glimpse of the multitudes and generations that will surely follow, knowing it is by small parenting means that truly great and eternal outcomes will take place.

{ Notes }

1. Gordon B. Hinckley, "Small Acts Lead to Great Consequences," *Ensign*, May 1984, 81–83.

Helping Your Children Become Spiritually Led

Wat if you were given the choice between a visit from an angel to your sacrament meeting or a sacrament talk given by your next-door neighbor while under the direction of the Holy Ghost? Which approach would you most prefer? Would this be a tough decision? Which mode of delivery would you choose for your children to be instructed by? President Joseph Fielding Smith taught, "The Spirit of God speaking to the spirit of man has power to impart truth with greater effect and understanding than the truth can be imparted by personal contact even with heavenly beings." He then continued by saying that through the Spirit "the truth is woven into the very fibre and sinews of the body so that it cannot be forgotten."[1] Knowing that the effectiveness of the Spirit can bring more powerful results than even a visit by an angel should be ample motivation for us as parents to invite the Spirit into our instructions and interactions with our children, especially when we know that those moments the Spirit is present will be retained throughout their lifetimes and beyond. Let's discuss a few ways this might be accomplished.

{ Teach Them Effectively about the Holy Ghost }

First, I have found that teaching children effectively about the Holy Ghost and His functions is absolutely essential when it comes to their spiritual development. President Boyd K. Packer said, "True doctrine, understood, changes attitudes and behavior."[2] I have found, though, that helping children understand a teaching or doctrine is not an easy thing to do and will not usually occur by merely talking about it with them. Elder Bednar once said, "Teaching is not talking and telling. Rather, teaching is observing, listening and discerning so we then know what to say."[3] I have personally found that one way to truly teach for understanding where we can observe, listen, and discern is to ask our children inspired, open-ended questions, which facilitate a discussion about a particular principle along with the sharing of experiences, feelings, or testimonies. I have included a few examples of this below and will discuss this in more detail later in the book. Simply put, when there is discussion, sharing, and testimonies given on doctrine, the Holy Ghost Himself can bear record of the things that either we or our children have said, deepening their understanding (see D&C 100:8). Along with these inspired discussions about the Holy Ghost, it can also be helpful if we use an object lesson or two, which, if used effectively (never at the expense of the discussions and sharing), can help make spiritually abstract ideas more tangible, real, and memorable. I have included below three ideas that might enhance your discussions on the Holy Ghost as you make an effort to help your children understand the related doctrines.

Table Salt

This idea is taken from an experience that President Packer had while riding on a plane.[4] Begin by giving each child a small amount of salt on one hand. Ask them what they think it is. Ask them how they might find out what is in their hands. Let them taste it. Now let them try to describe what they tasted without using the word *salt* (they will want to say "salty"). Ask them how salt might be similar to the Holy Ghost. Point out that the Holy Ghost has a distinct feeling like no other. Take them to Galatians 5:22 and show them all the words Paul used in trying to describe and pinpoint this distinct feeling. (I have adopted the term *Holy Ghosty* to put in place of the word *salty*.) Ask your children what the Holy Ghost feels like to them. You might ask them, "How do you tell the difference between the feelings of the Holy Ghost and other feelings?"

After some discussion, you may want to take them to Doctrine and Covenants 6:23; 8:2–3; 9:8–9; and Mosiah 5:2 for some additional direction. A quote I have enjoyed over the years that does a marvelous job of describing the feelings of the Spirit comes from Elder Gene R. Cook. He stated that when the Holy Ghost is with you, "you will feel humbled. You will feel peace. You will feel confidence. You will feel repentant. You will feel an increase in your faith, an increase in trust in Him, an increase in hope and in love, an increase of light or enlightenment. . . . You will feel uplifted. You will feel the truth. You will have a desire to share. And lastly, you will have a resolve that '[you] will go and do.'"[5] At this point, you could ask your children to share some personal experiences they have had with the Holy Ghost, and then you could share some of your own (as you are prompted through your discerning, listening, and observing). You might commit them to look for the feelings of the Holy Ghost, inviting them to heed the promptings that come to them and report back with some of the experiences they have had in a day or two during scripture study or the following week at family home evening.

A Peacock Feather

You can generally buy a pack of five peacock feathers at a craft store for fairly cheap. Keep in mind, however, that if you are a husband alone at a craft store without your wife, you might get a few strange looks! At family night, let your children feel the feather on their palms. They will find that it is nearly impossible to detect the feather, even when the entire tip of it is touching their palm. Have them turn their hand over and notice the difference in the way the feather feels on the top of their hand. (If you have never tried this, it is a must.) Ask them what similarities they see between the feather and the Holy Ghost. Ask them why they think that Heavenly Father uses the still, small voice as a method for communicating with us. You might also ask what types of things you can do to better distinguish between the feelings of the Spirit and your own feelings. Have a good discussion with a few personal examples and experiences. A quote that might be helpful to use with the discussion is from President Spencer W. Kimball, who said, "Always expecting the spectacular, many will miss entirely the constant flow of revealed communication."[6] If you want to touch on reverence and its importance, you might include a quote that is easy to learn and memorize from President Boyd K. Packer: "Reverence invites revelation."[7] Another thing you could touch on is the Book of Mormon phrase "past feeling," which was a description given by Nephi of his brothers Laman and Lemuel. Nephi said that becoming "past feeling" caused Laman and Lemuel to not be able to "feel [the Lord's] words" (1 Nephi 17:45). You could remind your children that becoming callused (hands) with sin can make it more difficult to recognize the Spirit (the feather). You might commit them to live in such a way that the Spirit will communicate with them regularly and consistently, helping them to make needed changes in their life that are necessary and will bring greater happiness.

A Bottle of Lotion

A friend of mine shared this profound quote with me years ago as well as what I call the "I'm a Hottie Lotion" idea that I have used in many different teaching situations, including home. I found out recently that a copy of the book this quote was taken from, *Key to the Science of Theology* by Parley P. Pratt, was placed by Wilford Woodruff in the cornerstone of the Salt Lake Temple next to the standard works of the Church because of its great significance to the latter-day work.[8] Elder Pratt said,

> [The Spirit] quickens all the intellectual faculties, increases, enlarges, expands and purifies all the natural passions and affections; and

adapts them, by the gift of wisdom, to their lawful use. It inspires, develops, cultivates and matures all the fine-toned sympathies, joys, tastes, kindred feelings, and affections of our nature. It inspires virtue, kindness, goodness, tenderness, gentleness, and charity. It develops beauty of person, form and features. It tends to health, vigor, animation, and social feeling. It invigorates all the faculties of the physical and intellectual man. It strengthens, and gives tone to the nerves. In short, it is, as it were, marrow to the bone, joy to the heart, light to the eyes, music to the ears, and life to the whole being.[9]

As you can see, this is quite a quote with a multitude of things you could discuss. Along with it, you might create some products, like "I'm a Hottie Lotion," "4.0 Pills," or "Need-O-Friend," or you could come up with others. I have printed some labels of my own and covered lotion and pill bottles and then put them in a shopping bag. You might begin by telling your children what each product can do (lotion can make you beautiful in one use, some pills will improve your grades, and other pills can help you find a friend). Ask your children how much they might pay for each product. You will have quite a discussion, especially when the kids start to notice that people today pay some high prices for many beauty products that actually do far less.

After some discussion, share with them the quote, pausing to point out the products and give examples of each; let them come up with some additional products you could have created. Sister Sheri Dew stated once in general conference that "no amount of time in front of the mirror will make you as attractive as having the Holy Ghost."[10] You may want to point out that when the gift of the Holy Ghost is given to a person at the age of eight, a whole world of possibilities opens up as we seek to become more like the Savior and develop His traits and spiritual gifts. You might also mention that putting spiritual things first, such as taking time to read and ponder on the scriptures before doing homework, would help them do better in their schoolwork or other areas of their life because the Spirit is more fully present with them. I had a student a year or two ago who said that before joining the Church he had very little musical ability when it came to writing or producing music with his guitar. But after joining the Church and receiving the Holy Ghost, he noticed a distinct difference in his musical ability and attributed much of his success to this gift. I have had other students mention the fact that often people can tell if others are members of the Church and have the gift of the Holy Ghost with them by the way they look or act. The point is to have this type of a discussion with your children so they can get an understanding of what the Holy Ghost can really do for us. A few scriptures you might consider looking at that might be helpful in these discussions include John 14:26; John 15:26; John 16:13; and Moroni 10:3–5.

{ Take Them Places Where the Holy Ghost Is }

After inspired lessons and discussions have taken place where the Spirit is present and a greater understanding has been achieved by your children regarding the doctrines relating to the Holy Ghost, it would be beneficial to take them to places where they can feel the Spirit's presence and better recognize His influence. You will remember that when the Lord first called Samuel, the boy prophet "did not yet know the Lord, neither was the word of the Lord yet revealed unto him" (1 Samuel 3:7). It wasn't until Eli, the high priest in the temple, admonished him, "Go, lie down: and it shall be, if he call thee, that thou shalt say, Speak, Lord; for thy servant heareth" (1 Samuel 3:9) that Samuel had his communication with the Lord. Taking our children to places the Spirit is present can likewise help them better learn to recognize the Spirit's whisperings and to respond in faith like the young Samuel did by saying, "Speak; for thy servant heareth" (1 Samuel 3:10). Some examples of holy places where the Spirit can be felt in abundance might include:

- Temple sites and grounds
- Church visitors' centers
- Church museums
- Local Church buildings
- Church history sites
- Family History Libraries

We have noticed in our family that with careful planning on our part and a few sacrifices to take our children to some of these special places, we have witnessed many small miracles occur. One such miracle occurred several years ago at a Church history site during a family summer vacation. While I was talking with my wife about our summer desires and plans, we felt our children might benefit greatly from a knowledge and greater understanding of their pioneer ancestors and of the pioneer faith and devotion exhibited by the early pioneers. After talking with a friend, I found out that the Church reserved several camping sites for families at a missionary village located near the Church history site known as Martin's Cove. These sites were cheap and reserved for families for the purpose of helping families have a better understanding of their pioneer roots. After making a couple of phone calls, I found out that we could stay in a reserved family site for as many nights as we wanted for a meager cost. I will admit that this was not the most relaxing trip I have experienced, and there were not many rides or attractions to keep my children "oohing and ahhing," but this trip may have been one of the most memorable trips we have taken as a family.

My wife and I carefully planned each day and found stories that we read to the kids in the morning and at night. We also closed each night by singing "Come, Come, Ye Saints" before having prayer and retiring to bed. On the second day, we traveled up into Martin's Cove by handcart, placing our small children in the cart and letting the older ones take turns walking and riding (we had seven children at the time) until we finally reached the cove, about three miles' walking distance. Along the way, we stopped in the hot sun to rest and share drinks from the cooler. The kids kept commenting on how much the pioneers must have suffered on their journey and how strong each pioneer's faith must have been in order to continue on the journey. We also talked about the challenges our own family might have faced if we were coming west with the pioneers. As we approached the sacred spot where, under the direction of Brigham Young, the pioneer rescuers came to the aid of the Martin Handcart Company—a company who had suffered beyond description—one of my sons turned and said, "Dad, I feel the Spirit really strong here." Then he said, "Dad, what happened here?" At that moment, I felt a wave of the Spirit as I opened my mouth to answer his question. As I spoke, I noticed I had all of my children's attention. They listened, without disruption or distraction, as I related, with some emotion, the sacred experiences that occurred at that place.

Now, I could have told my children in our living room about the pioneers and shared the same pioneer stories with them. We could have still sung "Come, Come, Ye Saints" before going to bed each night during those same three days. But nothing was quite like standing there with them and feeling the Spirit bear witness of what faith and devotion really were. There was no poking, giggling, or reluctance on the part of our children to pay attention, because they were feeling the presence of the Spirit and then driving the discussion with their own questions, which I believe was the key to this sacred moment occurring. From this experience and others we have had like it, I have learned that we can do much to facilitate our children's understanding of gospel principles by giving them practical and personal experiences, not just talking about it. We should not wait for a youth or Scouting activity for them to have such experiences. The Lord said that we should be "anxiously engaged" in good causes and "do many things of [our] own free will" to bring about righteousness, reminding us that "the power" is within us (D&C 58:27–28).

{ Give Your Children Opportunities to Share and Testify }

As shown with the Church's new *Duty to God* (for young men) and *Personal Progress* (for young women) booklets, the leaders of the Church have recognized the need for young people to share the spiritual experiences they have had in an effort to help them recognize and better remember the fruits of their learning and their personal efforts to become more like Christ. In a recent general conference address, President Thomas S. Monson shared the following story of how one family invited their children to share experiences they'd had each night during dinner.

A few years ago I read an article written by Jack McConnell, MD. He grew up in the hills of southwest Virginia in the United States as one of seven children of a Methodist minister and a stay-at-home mother. Their circumstances were very humble. He recounted that during his childhood, every day as the family sat around the dinner table, his father would ask each one in turn, "And what did you do for someone today?" The children were determined to do a good turn every day so they could report to their father that they had helped someone. Dr. McConnell calls this exercise his father's most valuable legacy, for that expectation and those words inspired him and his siblings to help others throughout their lives. As they grew and matured, their motivation for providing service changed to an inner desire to help others.[11]

In our home, we have experimented with different forms of sharing where our children have had opportunities to teach and testify to one another. Here are just a few ideas we have found beneficial:

- During family scripture study, have each member of the family share a scripture that has touched them in some way during the week (this can help change the way your children read their scriptures because they will be looking for something to share during the week).

- Choose a child every so often to pick a favorite scripture story to share as part of family home evening or during scripture study and relate to the family how the story is meaningful to that child.

- You could ask questions similar to the one President Monson demonstrated: Did anyone get a prompting today? Did anyone get an answer to a prayer today? Did anyone feel the Holy Ghost today? Did anyone have a chance to help someone today? These questions could be asked at dinnertime, prayer time, scripture study, or casually when you are tucking your children in bed at night. Rotating questions for variety and asking them every now and then so you don't come off as being too preachy or forceful is usually the best approach.

You will find as your children share and testify that not only will your children began to be more observant of the Lord's hand in their lives, but they will also, during the process of looking for spiritual experiences, learn to feel what it's like to be guided and led by the Spirit. You will also find that your children will begin to share their experiences without being asked to do so, which will bring about some sweet moments for you as a parent and give you further opportunities to teach them. One day, my daughter returned home from school and sought me out to tell me she had just had an experience with the Holy Ghost. She was fearful of dogs at this time in her life and had just been chased by a big one during her walk home. She smiled at me and said, "Daddy, I was running as hard as I could, but the dog was running faster than me and had left his master. As I ran, I wondered what I should do and prayed in my mind for help. I had the thought to stop running, turn around, and face the dog, saying, 'Hi,' followed by his name, 'Peaches,' just like his master had been doing. Daddy, I was so scared, but I decided to follow the Holy Ghost anyway. I turned around, faced Peaches, and then, as calmly as I could, I patted my legs with my hands and said, 'Hi, Peaches!' Peaches stopped, looked at me, wagged his tail, and then turned around and headed back to his master." As you can imagine, this was a sweet exchange between us, and I felt inner gratitude for how the Lord can protect us when we are seeking to know His will for us and act on those things we receive, as she had done. I was also grateful that she had learned how to recognize the familiar voice of the Spirit and was confident that by following His prompting, things would end up all right. Sister Julie Beck, general Relief Society president, said, "The ability to qualify for, receive, and act on personal revelation is the single most important skill that can be acquired in this life."[12] Think of the time, money, and effort we sometimes spend as parents helping our children become good at a sport or an activity or a particular musical instrument. These are not bad pursuits, and we are taught to develop our talents and improve ourselves, but in doing so, we should also remember to help our children develop the most important skill on earth: learning to feel and recognize the Spirit. I close this chapter with the following story taken from the book of

Jacob in the Book of Mormon that I believe captures the essence of the things we have been discussing:

> And now it came to pass after some years had passed away, there came a man among the people of Nephi, whose name was Sherem.
>
> And it came to pass that he began to preach among the people, and to declare unto them that there should be no Christ. And he preached many things which were flattering unto the people; and this he did that he might overthrow the doctrine of Christ.
>
> And he labored diligently that he might lead away the hearts of the people, insomuch that he did lead away many hearts; and he knowing that I, Jacob, had faith in Christ who should come, he sought much opportunity that he might come unto me.
>
> And he was learned, that he had a perfect knowledge of the language of the people; wherefore, he could use much flattery, and much power of speech, according to the power of the devil.
>
> And he had hope to shake me from the faith, notwithstanding the many revelations and the many things which I had seen concerning these things; for I truly had seen angels, and they had ministered unto me. And also, I had heard the voice of the Lord speaking unto me in very word, from time to time; wherefore, I could not be shaken. (Jacob 7:1–5)

You will note in the passage that it wasn't the *one* experience or even the *few* experiences Jacob had that brought him the strength to withstand the anti-Christ Sherem, but it was the *many* revelations and the "*many* things which [he] had seen concerning these things" that allowed him to "not be shaken." Let us as parents never forget this powerful principle and seek, as our greatest goal, to help our children become spiritually self-reliant through *many* different means so they will ultimately become all they should and can be with the Lord's direction and be able to weather the storms they will face during their sojourn on earth.

{ Notes }

1. Joseph Fielding Smith, *Doctrines of Salvation*, edited by Bruce R. McConkie, 3 vols. (Salt Lake City: Deseret Book, 1954), 1:47–48; quoted in Dallin H. Oaks, "Teaching and Learning by the Spirit," *Ensign*, March 1997.

2. Boyd K. Packer, "Little Children," *Ensign*, November 1986.
3. David A. Bednar, Broadcast to Seminaries and Institutes of Religion, August 2011.
4. Boyd K. Packer, *Teach Ye Diligently* (Salt Lake City: Deseret Book, 1975), 60–61.
5. Gene R. Cook, *Teaching by the Spirit* (Salt Lake City: Deseret Book, 2000), 200.
6. Spencer W. Kimball, in Conference Report, Munich Germany Area Conference, 1973, 77; quoted in Graham W. Doxey, "The Voice Is Still Small," *Ensign*, November 1991.
7. Boyd K. Packer, "Reverence Invites Revelation," *Ensign*, November 1991.
8. Parley P. Pratt, *Key to the Science of Theology* (Salt Lake City: Deseret Book, 1965), "Foreword."
9. Ibid., 101.
10. Sheri L. Dew, "It Is Not Good for Man or Woman to Be Alone," *Ensign*, November 2001.
11. Thomas S. Monson, "What Have I Done for Someone Today?" *Ensign*, November 2009.
12. Julie B. Beck, "'And upon the Handmaids in Those Days Will I Pour Out My Spirit,'" *Ensign*, May 2010.

Taking Advantage of Teaching
Moments in the Home

Years ago, a student of mine visited Jerusalem with her parents and returned home in awe, not just from the historical sites they had visited, but more particularly with the shepherds and the sheep they had seen along the way. One day, they were driving and came across an enormous group of sheep that covered the road for a great distance ahead. At the center of this large contingent of sheep stood two shepherds who appeared to be enjoying a leisure day, talking with one another without a care in the world. *How will we ever pass?* she thought. Then the shepherds turned, glanced in the direction of their car, bid farewell to each other, and began walking in the opposite directions. To her and her parents' amazement, the sea of sheep that flooded the road began to perfectly separate, like the waters of the Red Sea had done for Moses, with each sheep following its shepherd. It was as if that were the only thing in the world they wanted to do. The road was cleared in record time! She was in disbelief and bewilderment at what she had seen, and she gained a greater appreciation for what it truly meant to be a shepherd.

In John 10, the Savior makes some powerful connections about shepherding that I think are worth reviewing:

> I am the good shepherd: the good shepherd giveth his life for the sheep. But he that is an hireling, and not the shepherd, whose own the sheep are not, seeth the wolf coming, and leaveth the sheep, and fleeth: and the wolf catcheth them, and scattereth the sheep. . . . I am the good shepherd, and know my sheep, and am known of mine. (John 10:11–12, 14)

I love the description in these verses of the relationship we can and should have with the Savior and of His personal love and dedication to each of us, being the "good shepherd" who is willing to give His life for us. It is also impressive to note that the sheep *know* the shepherd and, it appears, desire to follow him, largely because they understand he knows and cares for them and will never leave them, no matter the cost. Sheepherders, however, care little for the sheep and are motivated primarily by outside forces, such as their own comfort and time or the wages they'll earn. The sheepherder's sheep are motivated largely by fear for their own safety and not by any personal attachment or connection to the sheepherder. I have personally found that as I have sought to be like a shepherd and forge a strong relationship with each of my children, helping them to see I love them and care to know them and am willing to give my life— or in other words, my time and energy—for them, my instructions and teachings are much more likely to be received. I believe in most cases, like the sheep in the story, our children will follow us without a lot of forced coaxing or forced teaching on our part when they see us as shepherds and not as sheepherders. Let me give you some specific examples to further clarify what I mean. I will use what I call "sheepherder techniques" as opposed to "shepherd techniques." I invite you to give some thoughtful consideration to other situations in your home where "shepherding techniques" may apply.

Example #1: Gathering the Family for Scripture Study

Sheepherder

- Yell or get angry about how slowly your children respond, expecting them to come at your request, with little respect for them or their time.
- Tell your children they had better get their scriptures or else!
- Say to your children that you are holding scripture study as a family merely because the prophet asked us to and they will be punished if they fail to comply.
- Cause the scripture study to feel hurried or rushed because you want to get on with other things.

Shepherd

- Give your children some time to finish the things they are working on, being respectful of their time.
- Invite them to bring their scriptures under the assumption that the Lord is going to teach them. Remind them that the family is reading together because of a love for Heavenly Father and that the scriptures are one way to be close to Him.
- Take appropriate time to discuss the scriptures without feeling rushed. Let them ask questions, and don't focus on the number of pages but rather what is going on in their hearts and minds. Adapt the discussion accordingly.

Example #2: Planning a Family Vacation

Sheepherder

- Make all the plans for what the family will do each day without any input or suggestions on the part of the children.

- Expect the vacation to run smoothly and then complain that the children aren't moving as quickly as you had hoped for, either in their packing, in preparations, or in the travel between places of interest.
- Make the decisions on the trip based on convenience or what you enjoy doing most. Put little effort or thought into what others might enjoy or what would be the best thing for the family.

Shepherd

- Allow your children to help you make the plans, and try to take into consideration every child's hopes and desires during the trip.
- Put an emphasis on quality time together rather than quantity time, where you can be together and enjoy each other's company. Don't focus so much on the amount of things you plan to see or do as much as on the best things you could see or do.
- Give the children a portion of the trip to plan, including some of the meals, and allow them to take an active part in the trip. Review the plan with them so they know what is expected of them and what the family has agreed on.

These are just a couple examples. With some thought, you should be able to come up with several others. The main idea is to conduct yourself as a parent in a manner that will help instill feelings of love, respect, and trust so that your children will be more likely to see you as a shepherd and be influenced by you. Some additional questions you might consider asking yourself might include:

- Do I really *know* them?
- Do they *know* me?
- Am I someone they want to follow?
- I would give my life for them, but do I give my time and energy to them?

These are difficult questions to answer, but I believe they are worth thoughtful consideration with a humble desire to change if need be. Remember that we may also need to adapt to our growing families over time, and realize that just because something has worked for us in the past doesn't mean it should stay a constant if there is something better on the horizon.

During my teenage years, my mother was good at having a small plate of food prepared in the late evening for my return home from a date or a late shift at work. I remember feeling appreciated and loved by her sacrifice and would often find myself sharing the details of my day with her, talking and eating while she listened intently with little interruption. Often, these talks would become great learning moments for me, as she would sometimes, after listening to me recite my activities of the day, respond with a little piece of counsel or advice that was just what I needed. As I look back now, I realize that Mom was—like a shepherd—making an effort to know me, letting me feel that she cared about me, and finding a way to help influence me in a way that worked for me and for her. Surely this wasn't an easy thing for her, waiting up for me or for my brother or sisters who came home at varying intervals, but I will be forever grateful for those late-evening talks with my mother that I'm sure have influenced my life more than I realize.

My father, on the other hand, had a somewhat different style of shepherding, which was also effective. He was an administrator and principal in the public school system as well as the bishop for a time in our ward growing up. He certainly had much to teach me, but I always sensed he was careful and cautious not to give me too much advice or lecture me into seeing things his way. He would instead give me little helps or encouragement along the way, mostly when I asked for it, and would then wait for me to approach him when I needed more direction or counsel. I remember asking him once as a young man to tell me what he thought was the best way to prepare for a full-time mission, and he responded with some sound advice that greatly blessed me.

As I have sought to know my children better and facilitate more opportunities for teaching moments with them, I have found Alma's counsel to be true that by "small and simple things" (Alma 37:6), great things can truly occur. Here are a few suggestions of some small things I have tried that might help increase the quality and quantity of teaching moments with your children.

- **"I'm running to the store. Want to come?"** I like to take turns asking the kids if they would like to go with me on errands to the store or other places (with the radio and all digital devices off, of course). I have had many great teaching moments when I have simply asked my children about their day during those drives and just listened to them with the intent to understand.

- **Monthly interviews**. These are a little more formal. During these short interviews, we sit down with each of our children and give them the money they have earned the previous month and ask them about the goals they have set. We like to always end by asking, "Is there anything you want to talk to us about?" Sometimes we have even asked how we are doing as parents or how can we do better to help them. We then will have a prayer with them, centered completely on them and the help that they need, and let them pick who will give it.

- **Dinner table conversations**. On occasion, as mentioned in chapter three, we have asked things like: "Did anyone have a prayer answered today?" "Did anyone feel the Holy Ghost today?" "Did anyone have a spiritual experience?" "Did anyone perform or see an act of kindness today?"

- **Bedtimes**. One good rule of thumb for bedtimes is to take time to tuck them in bed, and don't appear rushed or in a hurry! Often, when the day winds down and you come to them personally, they will feel loved and cared about and will share things that they may not at other times during the day. By taking the time to tuck them in, you will have time to read them a story if needed or take a little extra time to talk to the ones that need some extra attention.

- **Read scriptures with them**. On a rare occasion, I have personally sat down and read scriptures with some of my children. I don't force it; I just ask if they would like me to join them in their personal scripture study that day if I have felt they need some extra attention. During these times, they tend to ask a lot of questions, allowing us to talk more personally and learn more from one another.

- **When you're home, you're home.** As much as you find yourself wanting to sit down after returning home from work and turn on the television or hide out in another room, don't do it! This can be an effective time to walk around the house and see how everyone is doing. If you aren't ready to put on the "parent hat" yet, you may need to take another loop around the block before pulling in the driveway, which I will admit to doing on a few occasions. Find moments when you can relax and unwind in the early morning hours or later in the evening when the children have settled down so that as much as possible, they will feel you are there for them if they need you. Certainly this isn't always doable, but you will find that the more you try to free yourself up, the more your children will come to you with their needs or just to enjoy your company.

{ Don't Overschedule Your Family }

As our family has grown, being careful not to overschedule our family has become more and more necessary and, I believe, in great measure is linked to the frequency and quality of the teaching moments that we have had. Elder Dallin H. Oaks has reminded us, "We should begin by recognizing the reality that just because something is good is not a sufficient reason for doing it. The number of good things we can do far exceeds the time available to accomplish them. Some things are better than good, and these are the things that should command priority attention in our lives." He further said,

> The amount of children-and-parent time absorbed in the good activities of private lessons, team sports, and other school and club activities also needs to be carefully regulated. Otherwise, children will be overscheduled, and parents will be frazzled and frustrated. Parents should act to preserve time for family prayer, family scripture study,

family home evening, and the other precious togetherness and individual one-on-one time that binds a family together and fixes children's values on things of eternal worth. Parents should teach gospel priorities through what they do with their children.[1]

This has proven good counsel for our family and, when followed, has opened up valuable time with our children, especially when we have honestly made our children's activities outside of the home a matter of pondering and prayer on our part and on theirs. I have learned, for instance, that organized team sports are wonderful and have helped our children develop many important life skills. But I have also discovered, after coaching more teams than I can count, that the decision to involve our children in such things must be carefully and prayerfully managed, as Elder Oaks suggests, or a family's time to do the most important things can be easily consumed. I have also been surprised after asking my kids about their desire to play basketball in a city league, with me as their coach, when some have replied with something like, "I don't think so," along with, "Dad, we have a hoop in the front yard, and I like when you play with us and we have games with the neighbors."

{ Consider a "Remembrance Room" }

Several years ago, I got an idea to create what I call a "remembrance room." In this room, we have placed all the things we just can't find a place for. This includes a small library, some game tables, chairs for reading or playing games, pictures containing awards and accomplishments, pictures of the kids' sports teams, pictures of fun outings we have been on, and pictures from the past, including old friends and family members, both living and deceased. We also have photo albums and personal and mission journals that the children have access to in this room. On occasion, I have found myself enjoying a fun conversation with one of my children, including a few laughs, about something the children have seen on the wall or that we have found in the journals together. Recently, I caught one of my older sons curiously looking at one of my pictures of a group of my old high school buddies on the wall. He wondered, after looking at the picture, where all my friends were living and what had become of them since our high school days. As I reviewed each friend's story, I told of one of those friends who had drifted from the Lord's path, failing to keep the commandments before later being killed in a car accident. While I related this story to my son, I could see sadness in his eyes and sensed that he understood how important it is to stay on the path of righteous living, recognizing that there would be many temptations along the way to hinder him. I did not really have to come out and say it, but he seemed to understand, I think, because he was inquiring, and he could sense my own sadness and disappointment with my friend's poor decisions as I related the story. If you have the space in your home, you might consider such a room, where some of these meaningful conversations and moments might occur spontaneously. Even if you can't, placing pictures on the wall, perhaps in high-traffic areas, and personal journals in places that are readily accessible could be of great benefit to you and your children in facilitating such moments. It could also help bridge some of the gap or distance that your children may feel exists between you and them because of your age differences. Having pictures and journals somewhere in a box in the garage or in an attic where they are never used or looked at would be a great waste, especially when there is so much that might be gained from connecting the past with the present.

{ We Must Take Them at Their Times }

I have noticed over the years that many of the greatest teaching moments I have had with my children have occurred when I was least expecting it or when I was engaged in doing something else that I perhaps felt was more important. Elder Richard L. Evans once stated, "In all things there is a priority of importance. . . . And one of our urgent opportunities is to respond to a child when he earnestly asks—remembering that they don't always ask, that they aren't always teachable, that they won't always listen. And often we have to take them on their terms, at their times, and not always on our terms, and at our times. . . . But if we respond to them with sincere attention and sincere concern, they will likely continue to come to us and ask. And if they find they can trust us with their trivial questions, they may later trust us with the more weighty ones."[2] A few years ago, while tucking my boys into bed one evening, I certainly found this to be true. When I entered the boys' room, one of my sons asked, "Dad, what tempts you?" I was startled by the question. He then said, "We have been talking about what tempts us, and we wondered what things tempt you?" I knew this would be a good time to teach them about temptation because they had asked the question and seemed concerned about it, but I didn't really feel like having such a deep conversation with two young boys at such a late hour, especially on a school night. I was also exhausted from a long day of teaching at the seminary building. While my body cried out against it, into my mind came the story of the Savior at the well, when He, even though He was "wearied" after walking a distance of thirty miles or more, had taken the time to minister to a woman (John 4:5–29). As I considered the story and its implications, I decided that this might be one of those "well" moments. So, as late as it was and as tired as I was, I decided to sit down and ask them if it was a sin to be tempted. There was a long pause before they began to answer the question as best as they could, and we soon began to talk and listen to each other with me trying to understand what was going on in their hearts and attempting to say the right things and ask the right questions. When we concluded our discussion, I had the opportunity to teach them about the Savior's encounter with Satan (see Matthew 4), in which He resisted all of Satan's temptations, rising above them and becoming our Savior. I then bore my testimony that Christ experienced each of our temptations (see Alma 7:11–12) and that all temptations could be overcome with the Savior's help. I also told them that though being tempted is not initially a sin, it can certainly become such unless we follow Christ's example and pay "no heed unto them" (D&C 20:22). Following my testimony, I invited them to resist the temptations that would come to them at all costs, hugged them, turned out the lights, and headed back upstairs, contemplating God's goodness in allowing me such a special moment and being grateful for the Holy Ghost in directing my remarks. Please keep in mind, I'm not suggesting that kids stay up all hours of the night or that we shouldn't have schedules as parents. But I hope this story helps to illustrate that if we as parents are not listening and discerning by the Spirit what moments we must take advantage of, then we could easily miss an opportunity that may not come around again.

{ This Is Our One and Only Chance }

President Thomas S. Monson has said,

This is our one and only chance at mortal life—here and now. The longer we live, the greater is our realization that it is brief. Opportunities come, and then they are gone. I believe that among the greatest lessons we are to learn in this short sojourn upon the earth are lessons that help us distinguish between what is important and what is not.[3]

Similarly, President Ezra Taft Benson pointed out thirty years earlier,

When we put God first, all other things fall into their proper place or drop out of our lives. Our love of the Lord will govern the claims for our affection, the demands on our time, the interests we pursue, and the order of our priorities.[4]

These statements are clear, direct, and powerful. How grateful I am for living prophets who speak God's will and, in this case, give us the courage to act in faith and focus on the things that are truly important in our families. Our Father in Heaven, like the Savior, is the perfect shepherd and knows and loves each of us perfectly. We can count on Him to be there for us whenever we need. He will never leave us alone. May we continue to feel His power and love more regularly and consistently in our homes as we seek to follow the example of the Good Shepherd, even Jesus Christ, and become great shepherds to our flocks and not just sheepherders.

{ Notes }

1. Dallin H. Oaks, "Good, Better, Best," *Ensign*, November 2007, 104–8.
2. Richard L. Evans, *Thoughts for One Hundred Days,* 5 vols. (Salt Lake City: Publishers Press, 1972), 5:114–15.

3. Thomas S. Monson, "Finding Joy in the Journey," *Ensign*, November 2008.
4. Ezra Taft Benson, "The Great Commandment—Love the Lord," *Ensign*, May 1988.

Enhancing Family Scripture Studies

I n the beginning pages of the Book of Mormon, we read of a powerful symbolic and prophetic dream experienced by the prophet Lehi. You might recall that in the dream, Lehi sees a tree containing fruit that is "desirable to make one happy" and "most sweet, above all that [he] ever before tasted," being "white, to exceed all the whiteness that [he] had ever seen" (1 Nephi 8:10–11). We later discover that the fruit represents the love of God (1 Nephi 11:19–23), which can only be found in and through the Atonement of Jesus Christ and which leads us, through our faith and diligence, back into God's presence, where a fulness of joy is attained (see 3 Nephi 28:10). Speaking of God's love and of the eternal reward promised to the faithful, the Apostle Paul stated, "Eye hath not seen, nor ear heard, neither have entered into the heart of man, the things which God hath prepared for them that love him" (1 Corinthians 2:9). Lehi sought for and obtained this most precious fruit. He then pleaded and encouraged his family to do the same, despite the many obstacles they faced, including the large and spacious building, "the pride of the world" (see 1 Nephi 11:35–36); the mists of darkness, "the temptations of the devil" (see 1 Nephi 12:17); and the river of filthy water, "the depths of hell" (see 1 Nephi 12:16; 15:26–29), that ran along the path next to the tree. With these great snares, temptations, and possible pitfalls, we discover that there is only one thing that would allow all who were truly desirous to partake of the tree to remain on the path and finally arrive and enjoy its precious fruit: the iron rod. The iron rod, or word of God (see 1 Nephi 11:25), is placed so as to keep those seeking God's love on the straight and narrow path leading to the tree. You will notice from the dream's great symbolism that clinging or "holding fast" to the iron rod and then moving actively toward the tree of life is the *only* way to get to the tree; there are no other alternatives! Speaking more plainly, I once had a student ask if it was possible for someone to go to the celestial kingdom if that person did not study the scriptures regularly and seek to apply their teachings. After considering the dream and its symbols and implications as a class, we concluded that it would be difficult to do so, not seeing any other possible paths leading to the tree. Certainly there will be allowances for those who have lived in other times in the earth's history where there was not same access to the word of God as there is today, including perhaps those living now in more remote areas of the world where the scriptures and words of the prophets are not so easily available to them. But for the great majority of us with access to both the written word and the digital world, there should be no excuses for not studying and applying their teachings, for as the Lord has said, "Unto whom much is given much is required; and he who sins against the greater light shall receive the greater condemnation" (D&C 82:3). Knowing this has filled me with both motivation to search and study the word of God as well as gratitude beyond expression for the standard works of the Church, including the Holy Bible, the Book of Mormon, the Pearl of Great Price, and the Doctrine and Covenants. It has also given me a profound love for the teachings of modern living prophets, which if studied, understood, and adhered to *will* lead us and our families to the tree of life, whose fruit is most desirable above all else. Simply stated, any other path we might follow or direction we might take as parents, or any other use of our time and energy during a given day with the purpose of bringing joy and happiness to our families by attempting to lead them to the Savior, will prove fruitless without His word as a guide.

{ First Things First }

So how can we make our study of the scriptures more powerful and purposeful within our homes? As you have most likely discovered, finding a convenient and scheduled time to participate in family scripture study can be difficult thing. Some families will get their children up at an early hour before school and work to study the scriptures together, seeking for the Lord's direction for the family before the day begins. Others prefer the quiet time in the evening when the phone stops ringing and the day finally winds down, no longer distracted by the many daily tasks that can monopolize their attention and make pondering the scriptures together difficult. In both cases there are advantages, and much will depend on your individual family needs and circumstances. After thoughtful prayer and careful consideration, make your decision, set a time, and stick to it, but remember, as mentioned previously, that your circumstances may change and you might have to adapt your time of study more than once as children grow older and circumstances change.

Ask Inspired Questions

Asking inspired questions is a difficult thing to master. But I have found that if properly done, it can greatly enhance the effectiveness of your scripture studies together. Take a moment and think about the difference between the following questions.

Example #1

- Did Joseph do the right thing to ask God?
- What do we learn from the Prophet Joseph Smith's experience?

Example #2

- Does Jesus care about us?
- When have you felt the Savior's love?

You will probably notice right off that in both examples, the first question is a yes-no question and would elicit a yes or no response with little thought, feeling, or pondering on the part of the hearer. However, the second question in both examples invites the hearers to search their memories for experiences and feelings associated with the subject, in this case being Joseph Smith or the Savior. Try now to answer both of the questions to yourself in the examples given, and notice personally the difference in the way that you feel and in the thoughts that follow. Asking open-ended questions that provoke thought, pondering, and direction of the Spirit, including strength to act, is at the heart of good teaching and learning. Certainly we have all failed at asking good questions, including those more practiced at it, but remember that it isn't about being perfect with our questions as much as it is about improving ourselves over time through patience, practice, and repetition. You will find that the more you attempt to ask good open-ended questions, the more natural it will start to become for you and the better your teaching will become as a result, both at home and at church. You will also find that asking good open-ended questions is one of the main determinates as to whether a lesson or scripture study session is a success and is one of the skills that separates a great teacher from a good one. Consider for a moment some of the inspired questions the angel presented to Nephi as he, after desiring to know the things his father saw, was shown the vision the tree of life and its interpretations (see 1 Nephi 11):

- "What desirest thou?" (verses 2, 10)
- "What beholdest thou?" (verse 14)
- "Knowest thou the condescension of God?" (verse 16)
- "Knowest thou the meaning of the tree which thy father saw?" (verse 21)

Now, notice some of the questions the Master Teacher, the Savior Jesus Christ, asked:

- "What manner of men ought ye to be?" (3 Nephi 27:27)
- "What think ye of Christ?" (Matthew 22:42)
- "Whom say ye that I am?" (Luke 9:20)
- "Lovest thou me more than these?" (John 21:15)

Now, think of the discussion you might have with your family if you were to do nothing but simply ask your children these same questions that are already provided in the scriptures. Along with specific questions, such as these, there are many questions you could ask on almost any night and with almost any block of scripture that could invite purposeful and powerful discussions. Here are a few:

- What do you think Heavenly Father is trying to teach us in these verses?
- Why would the Lord want this in the scriptures?
- Where in our lives would these scriptures be useful to us today?
- Has anyone had any similar experiences to those we just read about?
- Does anything stand out to you in the verses? Why?
- What was your favorite thing we read tonight? Why?
- What are we (or you) struggling with right now? Is there anything from these verses that could help us (or you)?

You will start to notice that when you routinely ask open-ended questions in your family scripture study, not only will your discussions go better, but your children will also start to develop their own ability to question, ponder, analyze, and discover answers in the scriptures. In other words, your scripture studies together as a family will really become a model for how your children can and should individually study the scriptures, helping them to become spiritually self-reliant.

{ Give Inspired Invitations }

One day, while we were studying the scriptures as a family and eating popsicles on a warm summer evening in the backyard, I looked down at my scriptures and noticed that we would be reading chapter 9 of Moroni. I knew we were getting close to finishing the Book of Mormon, and I was excited for this, but I also knew there was a rough patch of verses in this chapter containing the detailed descriptions of the horrors of battle and of men who were doing unspeakable things. At that moment, I considered skipping this particular part of the chapter with our fairly young family, but then I felt we should go ahead and trust that the Lord had put these particular verses in the Book of Mormon for a reason. With that thought in mind, I proceeded, rather reluctantly, to call on our children to read the following passages:

> And now I write somewhat concerning the sufferings of this people. For according to the knowledge which I have received from Amoron, behold, the Lamanites have many prisoners, which they took from the tower of Sherrizah; and there were men, women, and children.
>
> And the husbands and fathers of those women and children they have slain; and they feed the women upon the flesh of their husbands, and the children upon the flesh of their fathers; and no water, save a little, do they give unto them. (Moroni 9:7–8)

After reading these almost unspeakable verses, one of my children spoke up rather jokingly, saying, to my surprise, "Dad, if that was to happen to our family, we would be in trouble, because there isn't enough meat on you to feed all of us!" At that, a few of the other children laughed, and I prepared myself to scold them severely for such a comment, but I restrained myself, for which I was later grateful. Instead, I fired off a question I hoped would hit the target and invite the understanding and edification we were surely lacking. "Kids," I said, "you are probably right. But what do you think caused these people to become so evil?" There was a long pause, and then to my great surprise, a heartfelt discussion began to take place. After several responses, one of my small daughters spoke up and said, "Daddy, I bet those evil men stopped saying their prayers." At that, we continued to discuss the importance of prayer. Before long, we had come to the understanding and agreement that the unspeakable wickedness we had read about was in fact the result of the small sins the people had committed without repenting of them. This lack of repentance or focus over time toward righteousness had allowed Satan to get a greater hold of their hearts until the unspeakable had occurred. Now, at this point in our scripture study, we could have continued reading or even ended our time together, having felt that our time was effective because of the peace of the Spirit we felt. But remember the Savior's words that if any man would *do* His will, he would *know* the doctrine (see John 7:17). Hearing, understanding, and feeling are all essential components, but they will not be enough to get the gospel to the much-needed "knowing" level without the person acting in faith. You will discover quickly that invitations extended to your children during your studies together will be the most effective, meaning they will be the most likely to accept and act on those invitations, when the Spirit is present. This is because of the Spirit's ability to give them the desire and motivation to act on such an invitation, including "no more disposition to do evil, but to do good continually" (Mosiah 5:2). During some scripture studies, you may not be moved to make an invitation, or the invitation may be a small one. Other times, you may feel a strong impression to extend a challenge that you know is meant for your family. Be careful that your invitations do not come off as being too programmed, repetitive, or "cheesy," or that you are just doing it to check off another box. Your children will be able to sense if you are going through the motions or if you are being motivated by a higher source. They will respond more positively if they feel it is what God wants them to do and not just something Mom and Dad are coming up with on a whim. On this occasion in the backyard, I felt impressed to invite our children to take a little extra time that evening during their prayers to really think about who they were talking to and try to pray with all their hearts, both thanking the Lord for their blessings as well as repenting of those little sins they had committed during the day. The following day, we remembered to take a minute and follow up on their prayers and hear some of their experiences as well as further testify of the importance of being watchful and repentant each day. Certainly, every family scripture study has not followed this exact pattern or gone this smoothly in our home. But when we have made a conscious effort to extend invitations to our children, as the Spirit has directed, we have witnessed a "knowing" level on the part of our children that we did not think possible. Surely this is because when a person acts in faith over time to the inspiration they receive, they are promised to be given more of what our Father in Heaven desires to give them (see 2 Nephi 28:30).

{ Both Spouses Should Take an Active Role }

As a couple, we have found it helpful to take turns conducting the family scripture study. One of us conducts the study while the other looks and listens to how the children are responding and behaving, adds insights or comments to the study itself, and disciplines the children should the need arise (all kids seem to enjoy poking each other during scripture study, which I have considered to be one of the great mysteries of heaven!). By having one spouse be the second set of eyes during the study, you (the one conducting) will find it much easier to free up your thoughts and focus yourself and your energy on the guidance of the Spirit and His direction for your family, not on the many other distractions that will be present. If both parents are not available, an older child might help with the disciplining, or you may establish some type of reward system for those quietly and actively participating. The point is, whatever you can do to avoid losing your temper or getting frustrated during the scripture study will help the scripture study experience be better for everyone, and you'll be more likely to receive divine guidance.

{ A Treat }

On occasion, when our children have brought their scriptures to our family study and arrived in a timely manner, we have offered them a treat of some kind. I will usually make my way around the house to tell everyone that scripture study will be taking place soon and then give them a few minutes to finish up the things they are doing and find their set of scriptures to bring to the study. (Remember, we want to shepherd them, not "sheep herd" them, as we discussed earlier.) We have never made a treat an everyday thing so that our children would always expect a treat for doing what is right, but a time or two a week, we have brought out a treat or had cookies or something at the table while we studied. You will be amazed at how something small like this can dispel some of the initial negativity surrounding the study, and it will put everyone in a better mood to discuss the scriptures. Remember, if you give your children a time limit to arrive at scripture study, you must stick to it. If one child doesn't get a treat one night, it may not be a bad thing (this has only happened a couple times for us), because it will help ensure that your children will be quicker the next time, making everyone's experience better.

{ Use the Hymns }

The Lord has reminded us in the Doctrine and Covenants that the "song of the righteous" is a prayer to Him and will be "answered with a blessing" (D&C 25:12). This is the case with every sacrament meeting in the Church, where we in essence pray twice before beginning the meeting and pray twice before ending it. Knowing that our sacred hymns are not just songs but prayers that can result in blessings has caused me to avoid the temptation to talk or do other things during the opening or closing hymn in sacrament meeting. The First Presidency of the Church has said,

> The hymns invite the Spirit of the Lord, create a feeling of reverence, unify us as members, and provide a way for us to offer praises to the Lord. Some of the greatest sermons are preached by the singing of hymns. Hymns move us to repentance and good works, build testimony and faith, comfort the weary, console the mourning, and inspire us to endure to the end.

They continued, stating,

> Music has boundless powers for moving families toward greater spirituality and devotion to the gospel. Latter-day Saints should fill their homes with the sound of worthy music.
>
> Ours is a hymnbook for the home as well as for the meeting-house. We hope the hymnbook will take a prominent place among the scriptures and other religious books in our homes. The hymns can bring families a spirit of beauty and peace and can inspire love and unity among family members.
>
> Teach your children to love the hymns. Sing them on the Sabbath, in home evening, during scripture study, at prayer time. Sing as you work, as you play, and as you travel together. Sing hymns as lullabies to build faith and testimony in your young ones.[1]

These are powerful statements and promises, and you will notice that the directions and blessings promised are not contingent on whether we can sing well or even in tune! You might consider singing a hymn together a few evenings a week in preparation for your study. This will help to add variety to the study as well as create an environment as mentioned that will be more conducive to the Spirit. It will also teach your children to know and love the hymns so they can sing them on their own during difficult moments for strength, as well as help them more fully receive and appreciate the messages or "sermons" contained within them. You might also find it worthwhile to, on occasion, choose to sing the same hymn each night for a week so that the teachings within the hymn might be better remembered and understood through repetition.

{ Vary Your Location }

We have occasionally held a study in the backyard, at the kitchen table, and even in our children's playhouse with lanterns and flashlights. In all these cases, the scripture study was the most important thing that we were doing, regardless of where we had chosen to hold it, but a change in scenery certainly added a little something to the study and helped our children be more attentive, interested, and involved. Think of the many different places the Savior chose to teach His disciples in the scriptures, including on mountains, on boats, on temple grounds, in the streets, and in their individual homes. Can you imagine if every temple on the earth looked exactly the same, with the same furnishings, moldings, and structure? Certainly we would still go to the temple and have a great experience, but wouldn't you agree that the many differences in our temples enhance the experience? Doing whatever you can to enhance or "add a little spice" to the experience to make it feel unique will make for a better study.

{ Vary Your Study Methods }

In most cases, and on most evenings, you will probably want to read together through the scriptures sequentially, with each person in the circle reading a verse or two. We have found this simple method to be effective as long as we take time to ask questions, discuss the verses, and extend invitations, as mentioned. But every few days or so, it may be helpful to mix things up a little and try something new. Here are a few things you might try:

- After reading a verse, the person reading calls on someone else to read (some like to call this popcorn reading). The readers can read the whole verse or stop wherever they wish within the verse and call on someone else to read.

- Have one person read and stop at a particular word or phrase and let the others, without looking at their scriptures, try to guess what word or phrase comes next.

- Pull out a Gospel Art picture and tell the children that you will be reading this particular story. Ask them what they see in the picture. Have them look for the things in the picture that match the story.

- Read for a few nights or for a week about a particular topic. During the week of Easter or Christmas, for example, you could show a short video clip or two from LDS.org on a part of the Christmas or Easter story before reading the verses together and having a discussion on them. This site is full of good short clips on just about any gospel subject and can be a great way, on occasion, to begin a study together.

- Review and discuss a special scripture at the beginning of the week that might be particularly meaningful to the family. Spend a minute or two each night during or at the beginning of study repeating the scripture together until the kids have it memorized.

- When you have small children, give them the scripture reader (containing pictures and short summaries) and let them choose and share their favorite story as well as help lead the discussion on it.

- Invite the children to bring to study a scripture they have found particularly meaningful that week during their personal study. Go around the room and let the children share the scriptures they have chosen.

{ Conclusion }

In conclusion, we must be careful that we don't get overwhelmed with our family scripture studies and try to do too much or seek to run faster than we have strength or means (see Mosiah 4:27), but be diligent at seeking to always improve. We can do this by not seeking to hold long or drawn-out studies where every element of the perfect family scripture study is apparent. Rather, we can hold small, consistent, and purposeful ones where, above all, inspiration is sought for, keeping in mind that the power of the study may not always come in the way or in the time we expect. I have loved these words from Elder Bednar:

> Sometimes Sister Bednar and I wondered if our efforts to do these spiritually essential things were worthwhile. Now and then verses of scripture were read amid outbursts such as "He's touching me!" "Make him stop looking at me!" "Mom, he's breathing my air!" Sincere prayers occasionally were interrupted with giggling and poking. And with active, rambunctious boys, family home evening lessons did not always produce high levels of edification. At times Sister Bednar and I were exasperated because the righteous habits we worked so hard to foster did not seem to yield immediately the spiritual results we wanted and expected.
>
> Today if you could ask our adult sons what they remember about family prayer, scripture study, and family home evening, I believe I know how they would answer. They likely would not identify a particular prayer or a specific instance of scripture study or an especially meaningful family home evening lesson as the defining moment in their spiritual development. What they would say they remember is that as a family we were consistent.
>
> Sister Bednar and I thought helping our sons understand the content of a particular lesson or a specific scripture was the ultimate

outcome. But such a result does not occur each time we study or pray or learn together. The consistency of our intent and work was perhaps the greatest lesson—a lesson we did not fully appreciate at the time.

He continued by sharing the following analogy,

In my office is a beautiful painting of a wheat field. The painting is a vast collection of individual brushstrokes—none of which in isolation is very interesting or impressive. In fact, if you stand close to the canvas, all you can see is a mass of seemingly unrelated and unattractive streaks of yellow and gold and brown paint. However, as you gradually move away from the canvas, all of the individual brushstrokes combine together and produce a magnificent landscape of a wheat field. Many ordinary, individual brushstrokes work together to create a captivating and beautiful painting.

Each family prayer, each episode of family scripture study, and each family home evening is a brushstroke on the canvas of our souls. No one event may appear to be very impressive or memorable. But just as the yellow and gold and brown strokes of paint complement each other and produce an impressive masterpiece, so our consistency in doing seemingly small things can lead to significant spiritual results.[2]

We would do well to consider the big picture, as Elder Bednar has suggested, and remember that our small efforts can bring about great results over time if we are consistent and anxiously engaged and if the desires of our hearts are truly the welfare of our families.

Years ago, I learned a great lesson while teaching the chapters on Lehi's dream (see 1 Nephi 8–15) to one of my seminary classes. After we had discussed the symbols of the dream and the principles contained therein as best as I thought we could, I invited my students to leave their desks and hold onto a plastic rod of PVC pipe at the back of the room. The instructions were that they were, as in the dream's teachings, not to let go of or leave the rod no matter what, but it was ultimately their choice to leave or stay. After all of the students were successfully holding onto the rod, I began to coax them off the rod with various enticements, such as an opportunity to look at my wedding album, a funny video clip, or some other entertaining thing. I told them that if they did not leave the rod, they would never get to see or participate in any of these activities I had offered again, which caused some to leave the rod and others to wonder if holding on to the plastic rod was or would really be worth it in the end. As we continued on through the activity, I noticed one young lady who was holding the rod so obediently but appeared to be in great anguish. When I inquired about her painful expressions, she responded with, "Brother Schmidt, I've got to go to the bathroom BAD!" I told her she could leave the rod for this completely understandable reason and that her fruit would not be forfeited. Her bold response to my statement rang true to all of us that day: "Brother Schmidt, you told us not to leave the rod no matter what, and I don't intend to leave the rod until I get to the tree!" Now, I realize this probably sounds quite silly, and we are certainly not required to read the scriptures at the expense of basic human needs, though many of us will give up sleep every now and then for the sake of the word. But imagine what would happen if all of us approached our need to study the word of God with the type of determination and commitment this young lady possessed to hold to the rod under all circumstances and not let go, no matter what. Just as Lehi and his family experienced great challenges while they traveled to the tree, we too can expect distractions, temptations, and a variety of forbidden roads to be presented with the purpose of drawing away our attention and focus from studying the word of God, personally and in our families. All of these challenges and difficulties will keep us from the ultimate prize we most desire if we are not watchful and fully committed. Now for the dream's conclusion:

> But, to be short in writing, behold, he [Lehi] saw other multitudes pressing forward; and they came and caught hold of the end of the rod of iron; and they did *press their way forward, continually holding fast* to the rod of iron, *until* they came forth and fell down and partook of the fruit of the tree.
>
> And he also saw other multitudes feeling their way towards that great and spacious building.
>
> And it came to pass that many were drowned in the depths of the fountain; and many were lost from his view, wandering in strange roads. (1 Nephi 8:30–32; italics added)

May we never let a day go by when we have not taken the time to search, study, and ponder on the scriptures, individually and as a family, so that, like Lehi, our families will have the opportunity to partake of the fruit of the tree, experiencing the great joy and the multitude of blessings that will come from it.

{ Notes }

1. "First Presidency Preface," *Hymns*, x.
2. David A. Bednar, "More Diligent and Concerned at Home," *Ensign*, November 2009.

CHAPTER 6

Enhancing Your Family Home Evenings

There is a story told of President Spencer W. Kimball, who on a Monday in 1977 after spending the day visiting the president of Mexico and several other places of interest, including a celebrated cathedral nearby and the Zócalo Plaza, desired to attend a family home evening. He was staying at an elegant hotel overlooking the Chapultepec Park in Mexico City and surely could have enjoyed some extra rest and relaxation from such an eventful day. His secretary, Arthur, recalled that they "had seen the rich and famous, the ancient and the magnificent sites. Now President Kimball wanted to attend a local family home evening."[1] Brother F. Burton Howard, a stake president at that time from Utah, who was attending them as a Spanish interpreter and representative of the Church's legal affairs in Mexico, was asked to make the arrangements. After dinner, they joined the family of Brother and Sister Agrico Lozano for a family home evening. The Lozanos had a humble home, including a sixteen-year-old car parked outside. But that mattered little to President Kimball, who played "I Am a Child of God" and "I Need Thee Every Hour" on their piano while they all sang and enjoyed one another's company. His secretary later said, "Imagine the prophet coming to your home for family home evening!"[2]

{ We Must Get Our Hearts Right }

We might do well to ask ourselves whether, like President Kimball, we make our family home evenings a priority, despite the multitude of other things that can draw away our time and attention. Are you holding your home evenings together as a type of duty, simply to check off the box, or are you focused on making them memorable and worthwhile? In Psalm 24:3–4, we read that those who will ascend to the "hill of the Lord" have both "clean hands" and a "pure heart." This means that not only are we required to be clean by repenting often and by keeping the commandments (clean hands), but we are to do so with the right intentions and in the right spirit of doing it, becoming more like the Savior and our Father in Heaven in the process (a pure heart). Certainly, you can still reap some of the blessings for holding family home evenings even if your heart is not fully or completely committed to it. But I have found that when I have personally tried to see my family home evenings as a great privilege and opportunity and not as a hindrance, our family home evenings have been the most worthwhile, enjoyable, and fruitful.

{ Make Your Family Home Evening a Matter of Pondering and Prayer }

The next important step is to focus on the teaching and instruction during your family home evenings. Make it a matter of pondering and prayer. Years ago, I was reminded of the great importance of doing this. At the time, I had invited my seminary students to be in charge of a short devotional to begin class, consisting of a hymn, a prayer, and a scripture. My only real direction for the assignment was that they were to seek out the Lord and involve Him in the decisions they made, including their choice of the hymn and the scripture they would share. During one of these student-led devotionals several days into the term, a young lady in class burst into tears while we were singing the hymn. I had never before heard or sung this particular hymn. It caused a few chuckles from students as we all tried to make our way through the song. I quietly approached her to see if I could help. She told me she was "just fine," despite her shedding tears a few more times during the remainder of the hymn and the ensuing lesson. On her way out after class, this same young lady asked if we could talk in the hallway. After all the students had filed out, she declared, "Brother Schmidt, I just want you to know I had an answer to my prayer today in our class. Last night, I was having some doubts about the Church and was praying for help to know if what I was learning and have been taught all my life was true. While praying, I asked the Lord for an undeniable witness that the gospel was true and that this was the Lord's true Church on the earth. As I prayed, I decided to grab a hymnbook and open up to a hymn I was not familiar with. I then asked the Lord, if possible, to both cause and allow that particular hymn to be sung in our seminary class the following day." (Keep in mind that there are 341 hymns in the hymnbook. This was quite a request!) She then said, "Brother Schmidt, we sang that song today, and now I know that I am cared about, that God really does hear and answer prayers, and that this is His true Church on the earth. All of my doubts are gone. I just wanted to let you know what happened and to thank you for today."

At that, she smiled and quickly hurried off to her next class. I marveled at her experience, knowing that God answers prayers in many different ways. It's certainly not always the way we desire, but on that particular day, He chose to answer the fervent prayer of a troubled teen in a specific and dramatic way. On the next day of class, I pulled aside the young lady who had prepared the devotional for the previous seminary class so I could ask her about her devotional preparations. I was looking for anything remarkable or out of the ordinary that had occurred during those preparations. After my inquiry, the young woman smiled and said, "Well, I just did what you asked us to do. I looked over the scriptures and the hymnbook for some possible selections, and then I prayed for help in selecting what I did." I thanked her for her preparation and efforts and then shared with her the story of the doubting young lady who had prayed for a witness in class the previous day, along with the dramatic results that had come from her hymn selection. As I spoke, I witnessed tears in her eyes and a spirit of gratitude that filled the air and our hearts. I thanked her for being inspired and reminded her of how good the Lord had been to her. He allowed her to be an instrument in His hands to do His work. It was because she had sought His help that He had revealed His will to her. If we are to have family home evenings that inspire and bless our children, we will need to take the time to ponder and pray about what is best for our families and our family home evenings. We need to seek the Lord's help the way Nephi did while completing the tremendous task of building a ship to go to the promised land. The scriptures read, "And I, Nephi, did go into the mount oft, and I did pray oft unto the Lord; wherefore the Lord showed unto me great things" (1 Nephi 18:3). There won't always be one exact hymn, scripture, or activity that will absolutely need to be part of a particular family home evening. But when we involve the Lord in our family home evening planning, He will be more likely to give us the needed direction on those things that will be of most value for our children on a given night. I have found that we don't need to have long prayer sessions or to go to great extremes when planning a family home evening. What we do need is direction from above. It will often come in small ways, such as during routine personal scripture study, personal prayer, or conversation with a child. It may even come during your simple goings and comings, such as a drive home from work when you ask yourself, "What is the need for our family this week?" The important thing is to consciously and purposely make family night a part of your thoughts. I have found that just a few minutes of doing this during the week can pay enormous dividends when Monday finally rolls around. If neither I nor my wife has felt strongly one way or another about a certain activity, lesson, or topic for family home evening, then we just do the best we can. We pick something we think would be helpful to our family, or we let the children make the decisions, acting in faith that the Lord can magnify and expand whatever is presented because we have put forth an effort to involve Him.

{ Give Your Children Responsibilities and Plan Ahead }

Giving your children responsibilities and planning ahead for family night can also make a big difference. One way to do this is to have a monthly chart where the children can find their names

Family Home Evening

Month _____

Date	Conduct	Songs	Scripture	O. Prayer	Lesson	Activity	Treat	Talent	Talent	C. Prayer

and their assignments. Then they can prepare for upcoming family home evenings ahead of time. My wife has been good at setting this up and reminding all of us of our assignments. To give everyone a responsibility, we had to get a little creative because our number of assignments is ten. On the previous page is a sample agenda we have used from time to time. You will notice that it is basic and simple and contains the assignments for the entire month.

Having our list posted early gives the children time to not only personally prepare for their lesson or scripture but also ponder and seek the Lord's direction. It gives them time to work on their talents or prepare for a fun activity that might require a little extra time or planning. When children take time to prepare their assignments beforehand, family home evening will run much more smoothly and will be of greater quality, making the evening more enjoyable for everyone. This is probably because of all the hard work and effort by everyone in the family to make the evening a success. Monday is then a day that everyone looks forward to because it is everyone's family home evening and not just Mom and Dad's. You might also find it beneficial if you have the time to take just a few minutes to review the content of your younger children's lessons, chosen scriptures, and activities in advance. This will allow you to help them make any needed adjustments and better understand and prepare to teach and testify of the truths in the topics they have selected.

{ Fun and Variety Is Essential! }

Phrases like "Is it family home evening again?" or "Do we have to do this tonight?" might be good indicators that you need to mix things up a little. We have our set family home evenings with a regular routine of scripture, lesson, activity, talents, and a treat. But we have also found it effective on occasion to set aside our regular plan and be a little spontaneous. For instance, we might take a drive to the temple and hold our lesson on the lawn, or we might have the children bring their scriptures to family home evening and share a scripture they found meaningful during the week. Other times, we have shown a powerful video or a few Mormon Messages and had a discussion on what we could do to improve as individuals or as a family. Sometimes, we follow up on a previous family home evening invitation by letting the children share their experiences and testimonies of the particular principle we taught, and then head off for an ice-cream cone or to the park to play some games together. In each of these cases, inspiration and careful planning have been involved, as well as a spiritual message of some kind, but there has also been a lot of fun, laughter, and play involved, which are all essential to a successful family night and can actually enhance the Spirit's ability to be present and unite and strengthen the family.

The Prophet Joseph Smith may have been one of the finest examples of one who believed and lived this principle. On more than one occasion, he was found playing on the floor with children, wrestling with a friend, or engaging in some other fun or humorous activity or verbal exchange with others. In Proverbs, we read that "a merry heart doeth good like a medicine: but a broken spirit drieth the bones" (Proverbs 17:22). It is because of this that we must seek for play and laughter just as much as we seek to lift and instruct during a family home evening.

{ Prophecies and Promises }

I have found it beneficial for me to consider some of the promises made by modern prophets for those who follow the Lord's counsel to hold family home evening regularly and seek to enhance them. I have included a few here for your own examination. I will start with the oldest quotes first, followed by those more recent. Please note the similarities between the statements, the promises given, and the consistency with which those who lead have given direction on family home evenings.

First Presidency Letter, 1915

We advise and urge the inauguration of a "Home Evening" throughout the Church, at which time fathers and mothers may gather their boys and girls about them in the home and teach them the word of the Lord. . . . "Home Evening" should be devoted to prayer, singing hymns, songs, instrumental music, scripture-reading, family topics and specific instruction on the principles of the gospel, and on the ethical problems of life, as well as the duties and obligations of children to parents, the home, the Church, society, and the nation. For the smaller children appropriate recitations, songs, stories and games may be introduced. Light refreshments of such a nature as may be largely prepared in the home might be served. . . .

If the Saints obey this counsel, we promise that great blessings will result. Love at home and obedience to parents will increase. Faith will be developed in the hearts of the youth of Israel, and they will gain power to combat the evil influence and temptations which beset them.[3]

Heber J. Grant, Anthony W. Ivins, Charles W. Nibley, 1936

As an aid to parents in discharging this most sacred obligation and duty there has been established . . . a "Home Evening" at which time parents and children gather around the family hearth in social and religious communion. In this day when socials, parties, dinners, business interests . . . all tend to lead away from home associations, the adoption of a Home Evening is highly advisable. It furnishes an opportunity for the parents to become better acquainted with their children and for children to know and appreciate their parents. . . .

We commend the wards and the stakes that are making special efforts to make home life what it should be—a haven of peace, in which faith in God, respect, and deference for one another and loyalty for truth and righteousness are pervading virtues.[4]

David O. McKay, 1967

Homes are more permanent through love. Oh, then, let love abound. Though you fall short in some material matters, study and work and pray to hold your children's love. Establish and maintain your family hours always. Stay close to your children. Pray, play, work, and worship together.[5]

Joseph Fielding Smith, Harold B. Lee, N. Eldon Tanner, 1971

Well-planned family home evenings can be a source of long-lasting joy and influence. These evenings are times for group activity, for organizing, for the expressions of love, for the bearing of testimony, for learning gospel principles, for family fun and recreation, and of all things, for family unity and solidarity.[6]

Spencer W. Kimball, N. Eldon Tanner, Marion G. Romney, 1976

Family home evening is for everyone. It is for families with parents and children, for families with just one parent, and for parents who have no children at home. It is for home evening groups of single adults and for those who live alone or with roommates. . . . Regular participation in family home evening will develop increased personal worth, family unity, love for our fellowmen, and trust in our Father in heaven.[7]

Spencer W. Kimball, N. Eldon Tanner, Marion G. Romney, 1980
Our spiritual progress, individually and as a Church, will largely be determined by how faithfully we live the gospel in our homes. The most important calling of a priesthood holder is that of husband and father. The most divine station of woman is that of wife and mother. . . . Fathers should lead their families in holding meaningful family home evenings. Such experiences will build family unity and influence each person toward increased righteousness and happiness.[8]

Ezra Taft Benson, 1992
Family home evenings should be scheduled once a week as a time for discussions of gospel principles, recreation, work projects, skits, songs around the piano, games, special refreshments, and family prayers. Like iron links in a chain, this practice will bind a family together, in love, pride, tradition, strength, and loyalty.[9]

Gordon B. Hinckley, 2003
We have a family home evening program once a week [Monday night] across the Church in which parents sit down with their children. They study the scriptures. They talk about family problems. They plan family activities and things of that kind. I don't hesitate to say if every family in the world practiced that one thing, you'd see a very great difference in the solidarity of the families of the world.[10]

Thomas S. Monson, 2005
We cannot afford to neglect this heaven-inspired program. It can bring spiritual growth to each member of the family, helping him or her to withstand the temptations which are everywhere. The lessons learned in the home are those that last the longest.[11]

What incredible statements and powerful promises that each of us desperately needs fulfilled in our homes! You will remember that the prophet Ether in the Book of Mormon visited the wicked Coriantumr, telling him that if he and his people did not repent, they would "be destroyed, and all his household save it were himself" (Ether 13:21). He then prophesied that "he [Coriantumr] should only live to see the fulfilling of the prophecies which had been spoken concerning another people receiving the land for their inheritance; and Coriantumr should receive a burial by them; and every soul should be destroyed save it were Coriantumr" (ibid.). These prophetic messages given by Ether proved to be true. Nearly two million of the Jaredite people were wiped off the land, except for Coriantumr. After fighting for three days and sleeping on his sword, he finally beheaded Shiz and then fell to the earth, having been an eyewitness to Ether's prophecy and its complete fulfillment. This is an incredible story, especially when you consider the great odds that were stacked against Ether's prophetic statements. How many different results could have taken place, leaving a completely different outcome? I once sat in awe while I went through the story in Ether (chapters 13–15) and found thirteen things I felt contributed to Coriantumr's survival. One is that Coriantumr finally fled from the battle to save himself and those with him before Shiz pursued him, desiring to kill every last man, including Coriantumr. Think of all of the factors Heavenly Father would have had to be aware of for Ether's prophetic outcome to prove true, including the strengths, health, and psychological factors surrounding each individual fighter, the conditions of the terrain, the strategies used, the armor worn, and hundreds of other things. It leaves me awestruck by our Father in Heaven's incredible majesty, understanding, and omnipotence. Even if Coriantumr were to be strengthened far greater than any other fighter, to be the last known survivor out of two million people is still saying something. The Lord Himself said it perfectly: "Search these commandments . . . and the prophecies and promises which are in them shall all be fulfilled" (D&C 1:37). How grateful I am for living prophets and their promises, including those about holding family home evenings, which will all be fulfilled. The blessings of family home evening will be given for our benefit if we will follow the command in all "patience and faith," knowing that if we do so, "the powers of darkness" will be dispersed and the heavens will "shake" for our good! (D&C 21:5–6).

{ Notes }

1. Heidi S. Swinton, *In the Company of Prophets* (Salt Lake City: Deseret Book, 1993), 98.
2. Ibid., 99.
3. Letter from the First Presidency of the Church, April 27, 1915; quoted in "Family Home Evening: Counsel and a Promise," *Ensign*, June 2003.
4. Claude Richards, *Home Evening Handbook* (Salt Lake City: Deseret Book, 1936), 2–3.
5. David O. McKay, in Conference Report, April 1967, 133–35.
6. *Family Home Evenings* (1970–71), v. Quoted in Joseph Fielding Smith, "Bringing Up Children in Light and Truth," *Teachings of Presidents of the Church: Joseph Fielding Smith* (Salt Lake City: The Church of Jesus Christ of Latter-day Saints, 2013).
7. *Family Home Evening: Happiness through Faith in Jesus Christ* (1976), 3; quoted in James E. Faust, "Enriching Our Lives through Family Home Evening," *Ensign*, June 2003.
8. (Family Home Evening, 1980 — Spencer W. Kimball, N. Eldon Tanner, and Marion G. Romney)
9. Ezra Taft Benson, "Salvation: A Family Affair," *Ensign*, July 1992, 4.
10. Gordon B. Hinckley, interview, *Boston Globe*, 14 August 2000; quoted in Gordon B. Hinckley, "Family Home Evening," *Ensign*, March 2003, 3.
11. Thomas S. Monson, "Constant Truths for Changing Times," *Ensign*, May 2005.

Eyes to See

I remember being greatly inspired by a talk Elder Robert D. Hales gave to a large gathering of seminary instructors in 2002. He spoke about the opportunity he had to visit a ward in Palm Springs, California, on one particular Sunday. He was walking down the hallway to visit the Primary when he found that a certain Primary class (eight to eleven in age) was in need of a teacher. A young returned missionary was recruited to teach the class. After Elder Hales poked his head in the classroom to say hello to the children, they asked him to stay and teach their class. He accepted after seeing their "pleading eyes and feeling [his] heart melt." Elder Hales then spoke of the insightful questions the children asked. One girl asked, "What are you doing to be a good Apostle?" Her question brought tears to Elder Hales's eyes. "I'm trying to be just like you, a little child. Don't ever change. I have spent my life striving to be just like Jesus," he said, "to be 'as a little child.'" He then went on to teach that we sometimes forget the sweetness of being a child and believing as we once did and that we should "Come back to it, hold on to it, and never lose it."[1]

The Savior understood this same principle and taught it to His disciples when they asked who the greatest in the kingdom of heaven was. The story reads:

> And Jesus called a little child unto him, and set him in the midst of them, and said, Verily I say unto you, Except ye be converted, and become as little children, ye shall not enter into the kingdom of heaven. Whosoever therefore shall humble himself as this little child, the same is greatest in the kingdom of heaven. And whoso shall *receive one* such little child in my name *receiveth me.* (Matthew 18:2–5; italics added)

Later, in the remarkable account of Christ's visit to the people in America, the scriptures read:

> It came to pass that he [Christ] did teach and minister unto the children of the multitude of whom hath been spoken, and he did loose their tongues, and they did speak unto their fathers great and marvelous things, *even greater than he had revealed* unto the people; and he loosed their tongues that they could utter. (3 Nephi 26:14; italics added)

It becomes clear from these scriptures that our children can and should be both our examples and our teachers. We would do well to not only be grateful for these little ones but also take the time to study them. We should do this with the intent to learn and improve ourselves in the process, believing the Lord can give our children the words to instruct us at times. Yes, we must provide, nurture, protect, teach, and build up our children, but learning from them should also be an important part of our parenting experience. Elder Boyd K. Packer said, "One of the great discoveries of parenthood is that we learn far more about what really matters from our children than we ever did from our parents. We come to recognize the truth in Isaiah's prophecy that "a little child shall lead them.'"[2] It is my hope in this chapter to explore a few things we can do to be more successfully led and taught by our children.

{ Listen before You React }

I have found that listening before we react can, though difficult to do, open our spiritual eyes and ears and our hearts to the things our children can teach us. I wish in many ways that I were better at this. I am reminded of an experience we had as a family years ago while on vacation that helped teach me this. At one particular stop in our travels, which involved a gorgeous lookout of some incredible mountain formations, we got out of the car and walked to a couple viewpoints. When we got there, we found that one of my daughters, only four or five at the time, was nowhere to be found! It was a hot day, around 105 degrees, which only made things worse and increased our fears. Had she fallen off a cliff nearby or been kidnapped by someone? Had she fallen asleep in the unbearable heat? After a great deal of loud and desperate calling, many silent prayers, and more fear than I ever want to experience again, I found her where we had been searching earlier. She was quietly sitting on the ground on the edge of the road, hidden from our view by our minivan. It appeared as if the road had recently been repaved. Our daughter was fascinated with the shiny rocks the newly paved road had produced, piling them up, touching the black tar that accompanied them, and comparing them to one another. I walked over feeling extremely relieved but also upset at her choice of entertainment under such hot conditions. I leaned over her, bewildered, and said, "Sweetheart, what are you doing?"

She looked up for just a moment and responded with, "I'm playing with the rocks!"

"Sweetheart," I replied, trying to control my breathing and my temper, "we have spent a lot of money to come and see some important places. We lost you and have been scared to death looking for you. Now I find you sitting on the ground on an extremely hot day, playing with rocks and getting your clothes all dirty!" She appeared to think about my remarks for a moment and then looked up and said, "Daddy, I don't care. I really want to play with these rocks."

I began to feel my blood boil, which on such a hot day only made matters worse. I wanted to react out of anger, but I restrained myself the best I could, for which I was later grateful. As hard as it was (and it was hard), I felt the slight impression that I should try to hear what she was really saying to me. Several questions entered into my mind: Was I on this trip for me or for my children? Was I on this trip to improve our relationship as a family and enjoy being together in a spirit of unity and love, or did I just come to see what I wanted to see and do what I wanted to do? Could I have enjoyed good quality time with my daughter and our other children in a less expensive but more child-friendly environment? I recalled the words from Lehi, who commissioned us not to "spend money for that which is of no worth, nor your labor for that which cannot satisfy. Hearken diligently unto me, and remember the words which I have spoken; and come unto the Holy One of Israel, and feast upon that which perisheth not, neither can be corrupted, and let your soul delight in fatness" (2 Nephi 9:51).

This verse of scripture took on new meaning for me that day in the hot sun because of what my daughter taught me. Because I took the time to listen and not react out of anger toward her, I was in a position to be taught some valuable principles in a meaningful and practical way that could help guide our future family trips and activities together. Often, while planning such outings, I will recall these principles taught to me by my daughter that day. Looking back, I laugh now that it took an incredibly hot day, black tarred rocks, and a little child sitting in the road to teach me this.

On another occasion, we were sitting as a family in sacrament meeting, and one of my other daughters (being seven or eight at the time) took her bread from the sacrament tray and held it, refusing to eat it. This made several of my older children irritated by her disrespect for such an important event, and they angrily told her to eat her bread. She would not comply with their urgings and simply held her bread, breaking off tiny pieces and eating them. What would you do as a parent at this point? It is probably a good thing I was on the other end of the row and didn't hear what was going on. I might have turned to her and, with a stern look, said, "Eat your bread. Now!" I might have assumed she was taking away from the spirit and reverence of the meeting. If parents are listening before reacting, they might say something like, "Why are you holding onto your bread, sweetheart?" They would ask a question with an intent to understand. In this case, my daughter felt comfortable explaining her actions to my wife and approached her, saying, "Mommy, I am breaking off little pieces of bread and eating them bit by bit because I want to think about Jesus with every single bite. Mommy, would it be okay if I did that?" With some emotion, my wife responded, "Yes, sweetheart, that would be okay."

That day, our daughter reminded us of the importance of making the Savior the focus of the sacrament meeting. This experience has since led to many discussions we have had as a family over the years about the importance of reverence for the Savior during the sacrament portion of our Sunday meetings. Our children do not all hold their bread each week and break small pieces off to eat them. This, I'm sure, would create quite a spectacle. What has occurred is that we have all tried a little harder to improve our reverence for the Savior and His sacrament, in part, I believe, because of a child leading us.

{ Recognize and Seek the Benefit }
of the Gifts of the Spirit

The following picture of a stone known as John Allan's Crescent Stone[3] helps to illustrate what I believe is a profound idea. This stone had a tremendously profound impact on the life of President David O. McKay.

I believe it can also have a tremendous impact on our families if we understand the message behind. Many years ago, while President McKay was serving a full-time mission in Scotland, he was struggling with a longing to be home and lacked the desire to be fully engaged in his call as a missionary. While he and his companion were out sightseeing one day, they passed a building known as Albany Crescent. On the wall was a large stone tablet with these words engraved on the top: "What-e're Thou Art, Act Well Thy Part." This caught young President McKay's attention. He left the road and approached the building for a long and closer look. Having been impacted by what he saw and felt, President McKay, during the walk home, spoke with his companion about an unassuming custodian at the University of Utah who helped with the football gear as well as assisted players with their homework. He said, "I realized then that I had just as great a respect for that man as I had for any professor in whose class I had sat. He acted well his part."[4] On another occasion while recalling this same experience, President McKay said, "I thought about this motto, 'What [E]'er Thou Art, Act Well Thy Part,' and took it as a direct message to me, and I said to myself, or the Spirit said to me, 'You are a member of the Church of Jesus Christ of Latter-day Saints; more than that—you are here in the Mission Field as a representative of the Church, and you are to act well your part as a missionary, and you get into the work with all your heart."[5] From that point on, President McKay engaged in the missionary work in Scotland with all his heart.

You will notice from the picture that there are symbols below the saying. These contain a few interesting connections that President McKay may have also considered as he stood looking up at the stone carving. Each symbol corresponds with a number created by either a shape containing a certain number of sides or a Roman numeral contained within the square. This forms what has been called a magic square. By looking at the shapes on the stone, you will discover that when each row of numbers is added together, they will total eighteen. It's the same result with the two diagonals. If any number were to be removed or changed to another number, the outcome of all of the other sum totals would be affected. Each number in its respective place continues to keep its own individuality, but the greatest

contribution each number has is when it is within its proper place, affecting the whole or the sum of the other parts combined. Like the John Allan stone, our own individual families contain a lot of different individual parts, personalities, interests, talents, abilities, and spiritual gifts that can enhance our family as a whole when we seek to exalt one another into an eternal family of celestial beings. Too often I have seen parents, and I have been guilty of this myself, pitting their children against each other. They create more of a competitive environment where children compete for attention and feelings of self-worth instead of being celebrated for what they have to offer the whole family. I wonder if this happens because parents are not fully aware of what a particular child can offer the family or because they personally value one gift of particular child as more valuable to the family unit than another. We as parents, though not meaning to, may actually contribute to our children placing their talents under a bushel, as Christ warned against, causing their lights to decrease and thereby decreasing the light of the entire family (see Matthew 5:14–16). In the Doctrine and Covenants, we are told that "all have not every gift given unto them; for there are many gifts, and to every man is given a gift by the Spirit of God. To some is given one, and to some is given another, *that all may be profited thereby*" (D&C 46:11–12; italics added). We are also told to "seek . . . earnestly the best gifts, always remembering for what they are given" (D&C 46:8). It is important to see these gifts in our children and help them develop and share them in a way that can bless the family whole. I believe we must make it a point to carefully and prayerfully study about the spiritual gifts that are available to all of us. Below, I have included a list of the spiritual gifts that have been revealed and references for study. I have found it helpful as I have studied each of these gifts to think of people I know who have a particular gift (my children included), along with examples of when I have seen each gift administered. The list of spiritual gifts is as follows:

- The gift of testimony
- The gift to believe in another's testimony
- The gift to see the differences in administration
- The gift of the diversities of operations
- The gift of wisdom
- The gift of knowledge
- The faith to heal
- The faith to be healed
- The gift of discernment and the discerning of spirits
- The gift of tongues and the interpretation of tongues
- The gift of asking
- The gift of listening
- The gift to weep
- The gift of avoiding contention
- The gift of being agreeable
- The gift of avoiding vain repetitions
- The gift of not passing judgment
- The gift of being a disciple
- The gift to care for others

- The gift to ponder
- The gift of prayer
- The gift of bearing a mighty testimony
- The gift to behold angels
- The gift of charity

- Moroni 7
- Moroni 10
- D&C 46
- 1 Corinthians 10–14
- Marvin J. Ashton, " 'There Are Many Gifts,' " *Ensign*, November 1987

I have found it of great worth it to take the time to carefully study the gifts of the Spirit available and their full meanings and implications. President Henry B. Eyring gave some good advice on the matter:

> As a young father I prayed to know what contributions my children might make in the Lord's kingdom. For the boys, I knew they could have priesthood opportunities. For the girls, I knew they would give service representing the Lord. All would be doing His work. I knew each was an individual, and therefore the Lord would have given them specific gifts for each to use in His service.
>
> Now, I cannot tell every father and every leader of youth the details of what is best for you to do. But I can promise you that you will bless them to help them recognize the spiritual gifts with which they were born. Every person is different and has a different contribution to make. No one is destined to fail.[6]

Along with President Eyring's advice, we might also take the time to teach our children about the gifts of the Spirit by inviting them to see the good in themselves and look for reasons why they have been placed in their particular family. As they do this, they will find ways they can benefit and be benefited by each other.

Regarding the importance of developing spiritual gifts, Elder Bruce R. McConkie once said, "We're going to be judged in the spiritual realm by how many of the gifts of the Spirit we manage to get into our lives."[7] If this is the case, and if we are saved by grace "after all we can do" (2 Nephi 25:23), then this ought to be one of the great purposes of the family unit. We are to grow spiritually, develop the gifts Christ possesses, and work toward perfection and ultimately eternal life with our Father in Heaven by helping to exalt one another.

I marvel now as I look back on my own childhood and the room I shared with a brother two years my elder, who was different from me in many ways. We enjoyed different tastes in music, clothes, activities, hobbies, hairstyles, school subjects, and just about everything else. Our spiritual gifts were just as different. One spiritual gift he possessed was the ability to engage in deep study to seek answers to difficult questions he personally had. This was something that impressed me greatly as a young teenager, and I would often catch him reading scriptures in our room, sometimes for an hour at a time. After watching his example, I decided it would be important for me to seek my own answers through study. This eventually helped me gain my own personal testimony and love of the scriptures. My brother's strong work ethic and ability to seek and work toward personal goals (another gift he possessed) finally led him on to graduate school, where he received a doctorate degree in a difficult field. Currently, he teaches at a university. Despite all his successes in education, he will still call me on occasion for teaching ideas or help with technology when he is making a presentation, saying, "You're the better teacher. Could you help me?" I, in turn, have gotten in touch with him during my seminary lesson preparations when I have struggled to understand a particular meaning of words in the scriptures or the historical context or background of a certain New or Old Testament scriptural passage. He can speak and read several languages fluently. He reads and understands the Hebrew and Greek languages extremely well, including the historical context and background of the Bible, like few I know. We are still different as adults by way of personality and some things that interest us, but we have learned to use our differences to our benefit and not to our detriment. What started as competitiveness as children has led to our own growth and development as we have sought to "act well" our parts and learn from one another. Today, I think we are more similar than we are different. Certainly not all siblings will be as different as my brother and I have been, but I believe the differences that exist in our families can and should be a blessing and source of growth and strength, not a source of pain and conflict. The more we can help our children understand they are together for a reason and aren't expected to resemble each other but instead learn from each other, the closer we will be to giving them what they earnestly need from one another. How grateful I am for goodly parents, a brother, and four younger sisters who have helped in part to mold me into who I am today. Like all of us, I still have some regrets for things I didn't learn or take advantage of while growing up in my family. But I am eternally grateful for a loving Father in Heaven who sees things "as they really are" and as they can and "really will be" (Jacob 4:13; see also D&C 93:24) and then places us in environments where we can thrive the most if we make the conscious choice to have eyes that see.

{ Notes }

1. Robert D. Hales, "Teaching by Faith," *Ensign*, February 2002.
2. Boyd K. Packer, "And a Little Child Shall Lead Them," *Ensign*, May 2012.
3. More on John Allan's Crescent Stone can be found in Matthew O. Richarson, " 'What E're Thou Art, Act Well Thy Part': John Allan's Albany Crescent Stone," *Journal of Mormon History*, vol. 33, no. 3 (Logan, UT: Utah State University Merrill-Cazier Library), 31–61.
4. David O. McKay, in Conference Report, October 1959, 83.
5. Gregory Prince and William Robert Wright, *David O. McKay and the Rise of Modern Mormonism* (Salt Lake City: University of Utah Press, 2005), 7.
6. Henry B. Eyring, "Help Them Aim High," *Ensign*, November 2012.
7. "The Probationary Test of Mortality," Salt Lake Institute of Religion Devotional Address, 10 January 1982, 10; quoted in Dennis B. Horne, *Bruce R. McConkie: Highlights from His Life and Teachings* (Roy, Utah: Eborn Books, 2000), 284.

Finding Joy in the Journey

Have you ever had someone, generally older and much wiser, approach you and say something like "Enjoy your children while you have them," or "You'll wish they were little again when they grow up," or "Oh, how I wish I could go back and live some of those days again!" I love these constant reminders and both need them and appreciate them, but I will admit that there have been times when the thought *Will it ever end?* has crossed my mind, with little or no thought about enjoying anything, but I have instead been focusing on merely surviving. Prophets have spoken often and consistently about the need to find joy despite the challenges that we sometimes face. They remind us that real joy is attainable and right at our fingertips if we desire and seek for it. One such reminder came from President Dieter F. Uchtdorf:

> My wife, Harriet, and I love riding our bicycles. It is wonderful to get out and enjoy the beauties of nature. We have certain routes we like to bike, but we don't pay too much attention to how far we go or how fast we travel in comparison with other riders.
>
> However, occasionally I think we should be a bit more competitive. I even think we could get a better time or ride at a higher speed

if only we pushed ourselves a little more. And then sometimes I even make the big mistake of mentioning this idea to my wonderful wife.

Her typical reaction to my suggestions of this nature is always very kind, very clear, and very direct. She smiles and says, "Dieter, it's not a race; it's a journey. Enjoy the moment."

How right she is!"

He then continued by saying,

Sometimes in life we become so focused on the finish line that we fail to find joy in the journey. I don't go cycling with my wife because I'm excited about finishing. I go because the experience of being with her is sweet and enjoyable.

Doesn't it seem foolish to spoil sweet and joyful experiences because we are constantly anticipating the moment when they will end?

Do we listen to beautiful music waiting for the final note to fade before we allow ourselves to truly enjoy it? No. We listen and connect to the variations of melody, rhythm, and harmony throughout the composition.

Do we say our prayers with only the "amen" or the end in mind? Of course not. We pray to be close to our Heavenly Father, to receive His Spirit and feel His love.

We shouldn't wait to be happy until we reach some future point, only to discover that happiness was already available—all the time! Life is not meant to be appreciated only in retrospect.[1]

With these thoughts in mind, let's consider some of the things we might do to focus us more on the joys of life that so often get overlooked.

{ Thank the Lord for the Ride }

First, thank the Lord for letting you have the ride! Among the many heroes I have found and admired in the scriptures over the years, the brother of Jared is one of my favorites. Can you imagine being asked to build eight barges that are "tight like unto a dish" (Ether 6:7) to transport you and your family to a "promised land" you had neither seen nor had proof existed? The brother of Jared needed to figure out how to get air into the barges for the survival of the passengers, how to steer the ship in the right direction, and how to produce light inside the barges during the long and tumultuous journey. In the case of each of these difficulties, the brother of Jared approached the Lord in prayer and received the needed direction. After his own efforts, he even received a personal manifestation of the Savior Himself, face to face! The scriptures tell us,

> And it came to pass that when they had prepared all manner of food, that thereby they might subsist upon the water, and also food for their flocks and herds, and whatsoever beast or animal or fowl that they should carry with them—and it came to pass that when they had done all these things they got aboard of their vessels or barges, and set forth into the sea, *commending themselves unto the Lord their God*.
>
> And it came to pass that the Lord God *caused* that there should be a furious wind blow upon the face of the waters, *towards the promised land*; and thus they were tossed upon the waves of the sea before the wind.
>
> And it came to pass that they were many times buried in the depths of the sea, because of the mountain waves which broke upon them, and also the great and terrible tempests which were caused by the fierceness of the wind.
>
> And it came to pass that when they were buried in the deep there was not water that could hurt them, their vessels being tight like unto a dish, and also they were tight like unto the ark of Noah; therefore when they were encompassed about by many waters they did cry unto the Lord, and he did bring them forth again upon the top of the waters. (Ether 6:4–7; italics added)

We can see in these verses the incredible trust the brother of Jared and his people had in the Lord. This was demonstrated in their preparing themselves as best they could for the journey and then "commending" themselves to the Lord to take them where He needed them to go. Notice that the wind never ceased to blow toward the promised land. God will continue to move us in the right direction if we have done the things He has asked of us. Imagine the families inside those barges running together to survive when all the air in their particular barge was nearly exhausted, kneeling in prayer (as families should each day), and asking the Lord for help in transporting the barge safely to the surface of the water, where air was readily available.

We are told that the people brought bees, fish, fowl, and other animals inside the barges, which would have brought about some interesting living conditions (see Ether 2:2–3). Consider the condensed living area along with the various smells and maintenance the barge would have required, it being "tight like unto a dish." How much would family quarrels and difficulties have been magnified in these conditions? For most of us, a five- to ten-hour car ride together on a family vacation with air conditioning and a DVD player is about all we can handle! What effect would the constant motion of the barges have had on the physical, mental, and emotional well-being of each passenger? Ether 6:11 tells us that they traveled for 344 days in the barges before finally arriving at the promised land, which is an incredible feat even if the bees were fully contained! Now for a truly remarkable verse: "And they did sing praises unto the Lord; yea, the brother of Jared did sing praises unto the Lord, and he did thank and praise the Lord all the day long; and when the night came, they did not cease to praise the Lord" (Ether 6:9). From this verse, it becomes clear that singing to, thanking, and praising the Lord often and consistently was part of what allowed the brother of Jared and his people to endure all the turbulence, smells, crowding, and other difficulties of barge travel. In the Doctrine and Covenants, we are promised that if we receive "all things with thankfulness" (including large and small things and trials meant to strengthen us), we *will* be made "glorious" (D&C 78:19). We are also told that "the things of this earth shall be added unto [us], even an hundred fold, yea, more" (ibid.).

I have found that one of the ways that we can express our gratitude is to take time to kneel on occasion, like those in the barges, and offer thankful prayers regarding our blessings, our families, and our children. We can ask for nothing for ourselves, but instead offer heartfelt praise and gratitude to the Lord for the many blessings, large and small, we enjoy. And then we can teach our children to do the same. This will take practice, but I have found that with some persistence, it can pay great dividends and change the way unexpected challenges and difficulties are perceived. You might also occasionally take a few minutes at the dinner table or before bed to allow your family to share some of the ways they have been blessed during the course of the day. As you get into the habit of being grateful, you will notice that you won't really have to plan for such moments with your family; they will begin to happen spontaneously. In addition to doing this, President Eyring has suggested that we might take a little time each day to record in a journal those times we have seen the hand of the Lord during the course of the day, along with the other things we might usually write about, quoting the hymn, "It will surprise you what the Lord has done."[2]

Now, notice the great blessings we can expect as we learn to thank the Lord for the ride: "And thus they were driven forth; and *no monster of the sea could break them*, neither whale that could mar them; and they did *have light continually*, whether it was above the water or under the water" (Ether 6:10; italics added). What incredible blessings! May each of us continue to discover ways to make gratitude constant in our lives so that these great blessings can be ours. President Gordon B. Hinckley, some years ago, quoted a newspaper article, which stated,

> Anyone who imagines that bliss is normal is going to waste a lot of time running around shouting that he's been robbed. The fact is that most putts don't drop. Most beef is tough. Most children grow up to be just ordinary people. Most successful marriages require a high degree of mutual toleration. Most jobs are more often dull than otherwise. . . .
>
> Life is like an old-time rail journey—delays, sidetracks, smoke, dust, cinders, and jolts, interspersed only occasionally by beautiful vistas and thrilling bursts of speed. The trick is to thank the Lord for letting you have the ride.[3]

{ The Medicine of Laughter }

One day, while driving to the store with one of my young daughters, I pulled up to a red light. When I stopped, my little girl looked out the window. Seeing another driver with his car window rolled down, enjoying a cigarette, she said, "Daddy, that guy is smoking! That's bad!"

Thinking this to be a good teaching moment, I explained that the man may have grown up in an environment where smoking was acceptable and with parents who were smokers themselves. "We have to be careful not to pass judgment on those who don't live the commandments as we do," I told her. "Perhaps nobody ever taught him that smoking is against Word of Wisdom."

She shook her head in agreement with me, and I felt satisfied by my instruction, until the unexpected happened. Before I could stop her, my daughter rolled down her window, stuck her head out, and yelled loudly at the man, "Hey! It's baaaaad to smoke!" She rolled up the window, looking satisfied, and turned to me, saying, "I told him, Dad. He knows now that it's bad to smoke."

I was ever so grateful that the traffic light turned green at that moment. I sped quickly through the intersection before finding myself laughing hysterically while my daughter looked at me, puzzled and confused. It wasn't until she was older that she finally shared with me in the laughter of that day.

This is just one example of some of the funny things that can happen during the course of a day. All of us have these types of occurrences. I believe it is worth the effort to remember and enjoy them, as well as lose a few calories by laughing at and reliving them. President Gordon B. Hinckley said,

> We've got to have a little humor in our lives. You had better take seriously that which should be taken seriously but, at the same time, we can bring in a touch of humor now and again. If the time ever comes when we can't smile at ourselves, it will be a sad time.[4]

Not only is smiling at ourselves important, but I have also found that, when done properly and not at the expense of others in a hurtful way, humor can help to create feelings of unity, enjoyment, and togetherness within the family. This is illustrated in the following story told by Joseph B. Wirthlin:

> I remember loading up our children in a station wagon and driving to Los Angeles. There were at least nine of us in the car, and we would invariably get lost. Instead of getting angry, we laughed. Every time we made a wrong turn, we laughed harder.

Getting lost was not an unusual occurrence for us. Once while heading south to Cedar City, Utah, we took a wrong turn and didn't realize it until two hours later when we saw the "Welcome to Nevada" signs. We didn't get angry. We laughed, and as a result, anger and resentment rarely resulted. Our laughter created cherished memories for us.

He went on to say, "The next time you're tempted to groan, you might try to laugh instead. It will extend your life and make the lives of all those around you more enjoyable."[5]

Heber C. Kimball, counselor in the First Presidency to Brigham Young, once said,

> I am perfectly satisfied that my Father and my God is a cheerful, pleasant, lively, and good-natured Being. Why? Because I am cheerful, pleasant, lively, and good-natured when I have His Spirit. That is one reason why I know; and another is, the Lord said, through Joseph Smith, "I delight in a glad heart and a cheerful countenance." That arises from the perfection of His attributes; He is a jovial, lively person, and a beautiful man.[6]

Surely Heavenly Father—who is perfect, wise, all knowing, and omnipotent—must also have the perfect sense of humor. Surely He must occasionally laugh when we say our prayers, blessing our chocolate-covered brownies with fudge and sprinkles on top or our calorie-laden triple-bypass cheeseburger with extra cheese fries to "nourish and strengthen our bodies." He perhaps thinks to Himself, *You really want me to bless that?*

{ Don't Be "Too Tired" }

I remember reading a study once, claiming the human body actually functions on a twenty-five-hour day instead of the regular twenty-four-hour day we have all come to expect. I remember chuckling when I read this, thinking that if true, we are all experiencing a daylight saving time of sorts every single day. That might help to explain some of the tiredness we all feel. During these times of fatigue, we might do well to consider that it is better to be tired doing good things than bad ones. We will be tired at the end of a day regardless of where we spend our time and energy; we should make it a purposeful, eventful tired and not a wasteful, unproductive one. In the scriptures, we are promised added strength when we are doing the things we should and pushing through the fatigue and weariness that exists as part of the mortal experience. Here are just a few examples taken from the Doctrine and Covenants:

> Verily I say, men should be anxiously engaged in a good cause, and do many things of their own free will, and bring to pass much righteousness; for the power is in them, wherein they are agents unto themselves. And inasmuch as men do good they shall in nowise lose their reward. (D&C 58:27–28)

> Wherefore, be not weary in well-doing, for ye are laying the foundation of a great work. And out of small things proceedeth that which is great. Behold, the Lord requireth the heart and a willing mind; and the willing and obedient shall eat the good of the land of Zion in these last days. (D&C 64:33–34)

> For whoso is faithful unto the obtaining these two priesthoods of which I have spoken, and the magnifying their calling, are sanctified by the Spirit unto the renewing of their bodies. (D&C 84:33)

> And any man that shall go and preach this gospel of the kingdom, and fail not to continue faithful in all things, shall not be weary in mind, neither darkened, neither in body, limb, nor joint; and a hair of his head shall not fall to the ground unnoticed. And they shall not go hungry, neither athirst. (D&C 84:80)

> Therefore, dearly beloved brethren, let us cheerfully do all things that lie in our power; and then may we stand still, with the utmost assurance, to see the salvation of God, and for his arm to be revealed. (D&C 123:17)

We have all had moments when we were too tired to do something that needed doing or failed to respond to the needs of those we love because of fatigue. You have probably found, as I have, that when we fail to act in righteousness and become governed by our bodies, discouragement and sadness result. President James E. Faust years ago shared the story of a lamb his father had found and given to him when he was a small boy. The story continues:

> For several weeks I warmed cow's milk in a baby's bottle and fed the lamb. We became fast friends. . . . It began to grow. My lamb and I would play on the lawn. Sometimes we would lie together on the grass and I would lay my head on its soft, woolly side and look up at the blue sky and the white billowing clouds. I did not lock my lamb up during the day. It would not run away. It soon learned to eat grass. I could call my lamb from anywhere in the yard by just imitating as best I could the bleating sound of a sheep. . . .
>
> One night there came a terrible storm. I forgot to put my lamb in the barn that night as I should have done. I went to bed. My little friend was frightened in the storm, and I could hear it bleating. I knew that I should help my pet, but I wanted to stay safe, warm, and dry in my bed. I didn't get up as I should have done. The next morning I went out to find my lamb dead. A dog had also heard its bleating cry and killed it. My heart was broken. I had not been a good shepherd or steward of that which my father had entrusted to me. My father said, "Son, couldn't I trust you to take care of just one lamb?" My father's remark hurt me more than losing my woolly friend. I resolved that day, as a little boy, that I would try never again to neglect my stewardship as a shepherd if I were ever placed in that position again.
>
> Not too many years thereafter I was called as a junior companion to a home teacher. There were times when it was so cold or stormy and I wanted to stay home and be comfortable, but in my mind's ear I could hear my little lamb bleating, and I knew I needed to be a good shepherd and go with my senior companion. In all those many years, whenever I have had a desire to shirk my duties, there would come to me a remembrance of how sorry I was that night so many years ago when I had not been a good shepherd.[7]

In the Garden of Gethsemane, Peter, James, and John fell asleep after being asked by the Savior to stay awake while He suffered for the sins of the world. When Jesus returned to find them sleeping, He asked a most painful and penetrating question: "Could ye not watch with me one hour?" (Matthew 26:40). Notice that the Savior was not asking them to stay awake all night but instead designated a period of time during which He expected them to be watchful and alert. Also notice that when He returned the second time to find them sleeping again, the Savior made no more attempt to wake them (see Matthew 26:42–45). This must have caused severe regret on the part of Peter, James, and John while they later contemplated their inability to stay awake for the Savior during the most difficult and trying time for Him. They had "willing" spirits but, like all of us, "flesh" that was "weak" (Matthew 26:41). I too have felt regret, more times than I want to admit, when I have failed to respond promptly to the urgings of the Spirit and given in to the natural man in me.

While we learn to cope with the tiredness of life, here are a few strategies I have found helpful. Keep in mind that all of us have different capacities when it comes our physical, mental, and emotional abilities and that we are never required to "run faster" than we have "strength" or means (Mosiah 4:27).

- **Take a little time in the morning or evening before the next day to prayerfully plan your day, and then work diligently at it.** King Benjamin, both a king and a prophet, certainly understood how to manage both time and energy and counseled that we should do all things in *wisdom* and *order*. This suggests thoughtful and careful planning so we don't run faster than we have strength. It also reminds us to be diligent so that we might "win the prize" (see Mosiah 4:27)

- **Don't sit down**. This is a must, especially when you know that there are certain things that must be done and you feel extra tired. I have found that I am more likely to receive added strength while I'm standing on my feet, ready to act, than when I am sitting and waiting for some energy to come. I tend to sleep better at night as well.

- **Limit the distractions**. I have found it helpful to, where possible, schedule time to check emails, get on the Internet, pay bills, and so on during the times when the kids have settled down at night or early in the morning before they are awake. The other times during the day might be considered "family prime times," when it is usually best to not pursue personal interests or hobbies but instead focus on the family as much as possible. For example, if I were to leave the TV off when I returned home from work and instead help my children with their homework, it could not only help them to get better grades (provided I know what I'm doing) but also improve our relationships with each other.

- **Plan some personal time for relaxation and a little rest during the day.** Nights and mornings are usually best for this. One key is to not to let your mind wander on all the things you should be doing during your relaxing times. Give your full attention to relaxing the same way you focus on your family, work, and other pursuits, giving each their proper time and focus as much as possible.

- **Set aside blocks of time that aren't planned or programmed for whatever comes your way.** If you can do this, you will find yourself much less frustrated and annoyed when a child comes to you with "I need this for school tomorrow," or "Daddy, can you fix this?" or "Mommy, can I get some help on this?" I have also noticed that when I have had some of these unplanned times set aside, my children tend to gravitate toward asking me for help during these times, making everyone's life a whole lot easier.

- **Avoid using phrases like "I'm tired" or "I need to rest."** You may feel it, but try not to think or say it. It is amazing how much better you will feel if you try to avoid the thought of weariness.

- **Get proper rest.** There are many people who would never smoke a cigarette, but they will continually get less sleep than their body requires each night. Keep in mind that both are part of the Word of Wisdom (D&C 89; also see D&C 88:124), and both are essential to our success and physical well-being.

- **Take a little time to exercise every day.** When doing this, you don't have to have long, drawn-out gym routines where you are away from your family and focusing primarily on your looks. But you can exercise in small spurts if need be. You will find that twenty minutes on a bike or a fifteen-minute jog each day can make a big difference in the way you feel and perform at home.

Even something small like walking up and down the stairs several times during the morning or at night before bed can increase your energy and efforts throughout the day.

- **Pray often for help.** Heavenly Father desires more than anything to help you with your many righteous activities, especially when there is a need and you get tired. He will give you added strength when it is needed throughout the day if you will ask for it (see Luke 11:9-13).

- **Follow the example of the Savior.** How grateful I constantly am for a loving Savior who pushed Himself through fatigue and pain without measure or words to describe to carry out His mission! How glorious are the words He finally uttered on the cross, "It is finished" (John 19:30), having done the will of His Father in all things. I have felt great cause to rejoice in the declaration made by the angel following His Ascension into heaven: "He is not here: for he is risen, as he said. Come, see the place where the Lord lay. And go quickly, and tell his disciples that he is risen from the dead" (Matthew 28:6–7). In this bold declaration, I can almost hear the angel saying, "He is no longer tired! He did it! He did it! He broke the bands of death and now has a perfect, resurrected body, free from all pain, discomfort, and weariness!" When our resurrection day finally comes, we too will no longer get fatigued or physically tired. We will enjoy the eternities free from these physical limitations. What a marvelous thought! I hope it will be said of us that we too finished our work, pushing through all our wearied days and nights in an effort to build and strengthen our families. For surely it is better to be weary in well doing than in evil doing.

{ Finding Joy Now }

I close this chapter with the words of President Thomas S. Monson: "I plead with you not to let those most important things pass you by as you plan for that illusive and nonexistent future when you will have time to do all that you want to do. Instead, find joy in the journey—now."[8]

It is clear that the word President Monson wanted to emphasize was the word *now*. It is *now* we should learn to discover joy. It is *now* joy is available to us. It is *now* we will surely regret if we have failed to notice all the small and simple joys that surround us and that are the threads that make up the fabric of each day, and ultimately eternity. We should strive to go through each day with a smile on our faces and a song in our hearts, because it is then we will discover what true joy really is.

{ Notes }

1. Dieter F. Uchtdorf, "Of Regrets and Resolutions," *Ensign*, November 2012.
2. "Count Your Blessings," *Hymns*, no. 241; quoted in Henry B. Eyring, "O Remember, Remember," *Ensign*, November 2007.
3. Jenkin Lloyd Jones, as quoted by Gordon B. Hinckley, "God Shall Give unto You Knowledge by His Holy Spirit," Brigham Young University Devotional, 25 September 1973.
4. Gordon B. Hinckley, Interview with Mike Cannon of *Church News*, Dublin, Ireland, September 1, 1995; quoted in Gordon B. Hinckley, *Teachings of Gordon B. Hinckley* (Salt Lake City: Deseret Book, 1997), 432.
5. Joseph B. Wirthlin, "Come What May, and Love It," *Ensign*, November 2008.
6. Heber C. Kimball, *Journal of Discourses*, 4:222.
7. James E. Faust, "Responsibilities of Shepherds," *Ensign*, May 1995.
8. Thomas S. Monson, "Finding Joy in the Journey," *Ensign*, November 2008.

Establishing a Christ-Centered Home

For Easter one year, my wife suggested that each night before bed for one week, we read a portion of the scriptural account of Savior's final week in mortality and show the children a short video clip of each event, discussing any questions that arose. We found that this didn't take much more time than our normal scripture study, about twenty minutes, but I was amazed at the questions the children brought up, as well as the Spirit that permeated our home during our reading and discussions. At the conclusion of the week, I felt a more profound gratitude and love toward the Savior, having reflected much on His sacrifice and the eternal consequences that resulted from all He went through for each of us. Along with my own stirrings, I knew my wife had been inspired. I also sensed a deeper understanding and love for the Savior in my children. It appeared they had a greater desire to demonstrate Christlike demeanor toward one another. Since then, we have explored other ways we might "talk of Christ" and "preach of Christ" more in our conversations and lessons (2 Nephi 25:26), knowing that by building upon a foundation of Jesus Christ, we are promised great resistance against the storms of life (see Helaman 5:12).

{ Look for "Christ Moments" in Your Instruction }

President Henry B. Eyring once said that during his family nights, "I would find a way to encourage someone to testify of the Savior and His mission. Sometimes the parents did it. On our best nights, we found a way to encourage the children to do it, either by presenting the lesson or answering questions. When testimony about the Savior was borne, the Holy Ghost verified it. On those nights we felt our hearts being knit together."[1] I have found that one way to make Christ part of a family night lesson or scripture study, as President Eyring has suggested, is after discussing a principle, ask a question, such as "How did Christ demonstrate this principle or teaching?" or "What did Christ say or teach about this?" When our children have been given some time to ponder and reflect on the Savior, their responses will usually include a testimony of Christ. This confirms the truthfulness of the principle or doctrine that is being taught much more powerfully than the doctrine or teaching on its own.

Let's say you were teaching about the importance and necessity of prayer in our lives. You might use Doctrine and Covenants 10:5, where we are instructed to "pray always" to avoid the temptations of the devil. Or you might share Nephi's counsel in the Book of Mormon where he instructs us that "the evil spirit teacheth not a man to pray, but teacheth him that he must not pray" (2 Nephi 32:8). These scriptures would teach the doctrines of prayer powerfully. But let's say that during your discussions, you ask something like, "What were the Savior's prayers like?" or, "How did the Savior pray like this?" If you have young children or those less experienced in the scriptures, you might instead ask, "What do you *think* the Savior's prayers were like?" Take a moment now and think of how you might personally answer this question. Consider a few scriptural accounts that come to mind. I immediately think of the visit of Christ to the people in America and the Book of Mormon record stating that "the things which he prayed cannot be written, and the multitude did bear record who heard him" (3 Nephi 17:15). The account continues,

The eye hath never seen, neither hath the ear heard, before, so great and marvelous things as we saw and heard Jesus speak unto the Father;

And no tongue can speak, neither can there be written by any man, neither can the hearts of men conceive so great and marvelous things as we both saw and heard Jesus speak; and no one can conceive of the joy which filled our souls at the time we heard him pray for us unto the Father. (Verses 16–17)

Later in this account, the people tried to emulate His pattern of prayer. As a result, we discover they "did not multiply many words, for it was *given unto them* what they should pray, and they were *filled with desire*" (3 Nephi 19:24; italics added). At this point, as parents you could share a time when you were filled with desire to pray, or when you were given the words to say, and testify of how different a prayer is when it is given this way. Think now, and I include myself in this, of the difference you could make in your children's lives if they were to act on the principles of prayer found in these verses and in the testimonies you have borne. Think of the impact it would have if they learned to pray this way. Think of how their ability to feel and recognize the Spirit, magnify their callings in the Church, give priesthood blessings, and raise a family of their own could improve when they are directed by the same Spirit that "teacheth a man to pray" (2 Nephi 32:8).

I have always marveled when reading an account taken from the Gospel of Mark:

And at even, when the sun did set, they brought unto him [the Savior] all that were diseased, and them that were possessed with devils.

And all the city was gathered together at the door.

And he healed many that were sick of divers diseases, and cast out many devils; and suffered not the devils to speak, because they knew him. (Mark 1:32–34)

Consider for a moment how late the Savior must have stayed up before the last person was finally given the personal attention required; the last person was finally administered to with love from the Savior before Jesus was able to retire for the evening. The story continues,

> And in the morning, rising up a great while before day, he went out, and departed into a solitary place, and there prayed.
>
> And Simon and they that were with him followed after him.
>
> And when they had found him, they said unto him, All men seek for thee.
>
> And he said unto them, Let us go into the next towns, that I may preach there also: for therefore came I forth. (Mark 1:35–38)

We can see from the Savior's perfect example in this account the importance He placed on prayer. Notice too how direction came to Him from the Father on how He was to proceed during the day. He used His time and energy to serve best as He took time to commune with Heavenly Father. By using examples such as these or others found in the scriptures where the Savior teaches about or models prayer, you will notice that the discussions you have will become much richer. A deeper faith in, greater love for, and reliance on the Savior will result. To use an analogy from the Savior Himself, He taught, "I am the vine, ye are the branches: He that abideth in me, and I in him, the same bringeth forth much fruit" (John 15:5). If we apply this analogy to our teaching, we will teach gospel principles not as unrelated ideas but as appendages of the Atonement of Jesus Christ, as the Prophet Joseph Smith declared them to be.[2] This is how we make the Savior the focus of our instruction and not merely the leaves we have plucked from His true vine. If we make Him the center of our instruction, we are promised nourishment, strength, and growth, including fruit-bearing branches. Our discussions and lessons will have greater converting power and long-term results.

{ A Picture Is Worth a Thousand Words }

Another thing we have found that helps to establish a more Christ-centered home is to have pictures of Christ, the temple, and other gospel-related things where they can readily be seen. We want our children to know what is truly important to us. I remember early in our marriage trudging through several stores with my wife trying to find "the perfect" pictures, paintings, and wall decor to make our home pleasant and inviting as we started our lives together. After several stores and a whole lot of frustration, it finally dawned on us that a picture of Christ would be the perfect addition to our home. It would help create the feeling of peace and reverence we sorely desired.

A few years ago, while sitting with our children at tithing settlement, our good bishop invited our ten-year-old son to take a small picture of the Savior and decide where in our home to place it so it would be a constant reminder of our family's commitment to follow Christ. After returning home, our son placed the picture on the inside of the front door, where, he said, "each of us would see it the most." This has been a great blessing and constant reminder to all of us of our promises to follow Jesus Christ when we leave home each day. Regardless of where you place pictures in your home, it would be worth the effort to note the pictures on the walls and the messages you are sending to your children. Is the art in your home portraying the message that you are committed to following Christ?

{ Seek Consistently to Improve Your Own Relationship with the Savior }

Surely it does not come as a surprise to any of us that our relationship with our Heavenly Father and the Savior should be first and foremost. We should be constantly and consistently working toward understanding and fully appreciating that relationship, it being "life eternal" (John 17:3). Yet, often during the busyness of life, our busy schedules, or the next "important thing," we take little time to reflect and ponder on the infinite and eternal blessings that have been given to each of us. We forget the need to "draw near" to Him so that He might "draw near" to us (D&C 88:63). Elder Tad Callister has said,

> The Atonement is not a doctrine that lends itself to some singular approach, like a universal formula. It must be felt, not just "figured"; internalized, not just analyzed. The pursuit of this doctrine requires the total person, for the Atonement of Jesus Christ is the most supernal, mind-expanding, passionate doctrine this world or universe will ever know.[3]

Here are a few ideas I have found helpful as I have sought to "internalize" and "feel," not just "figure," the Atonement.

- **Mark and ponder on the Atonement scriptural passages in the Book of Mormon.** This can be a powerful and profound experience. This idea was first presented to me by a stake president, giving guidance to understand the Atonement more fully. This same pattern could also be followed using the other standard works of the Church: the Old and New Testaments, the Pearl of Great Price, and the Doctrine and Covenants.

- **Take time at the temple to ponder on the Atonement.** While at the temple, consistently take time to contemplate the Savior and His Atonement. Ponder your relationship with Him and His relationship with Heavenly Father. Elder Richard G. Scott stated that, if done, "this simple act will lead to greater understanding of the supernal nature of the temple ordinances."[4]

- **Pray fervently and frequently for help to understand the Atonement and its teachings.** Honest and sincere prayers coupled with a desire to know and faith in Christ is a great formula to come to an understanding of gospel principles, especially those principles related to the Atonement (see James 1:1–5; Enos 1:1–8, 11–15).

- **Study the sacrament prayers.** Along with a study of the sacrament prayers, you might also study the accounts of the Last Supper as recorded in the New Testament. As you study these verses, take time to reflect and ponder on each word or phrase and its meaning to you personally (see D&C 20:77, 79; Moroni 4–5; Luke 22:14–20; Matthew 26:20, 26–30; and Mark 14:22–26).

- **Set aside some time for additional pondering and meditation.** This can be done indoors in a quiet room or outdoors in nature. On one occasion, President Spencer W. Kimball was taken camping to recover from a series of heart attacks. At one point on the trip, he couldn't be found, and a search party was sent out to discover his whereabouts. Searchers found him several miles away beneath a large pine tree with his Bible open to the last chapter of the Gospel of John. In response to their worried looks, he stated, "Six years ago today I was called to be an Apostle of the Lord Jesus Christ. And I just wanted to spend the day with Him whose witness I am."[5]

- **Look for examples of Christ in the scriptures.** While you reflect on principles you discover in your daily scripture study and how you might apply them in your own life, consider the examples of how Christ applied the principles in His life. Doing this on your own will both strengthen your testimony of Him and prepare you for the discussions about Christ you will have with your family.

- **Testify of Christ on occasion**. Elder Boyd K. Packer stated, "A testimony is to be found in the bearing of it."[6] This can be done during fast and testimony meetings or at home with your family. Keep in mind that sharing your testimony in one place shouldn't compensate for not sharing it in the other. Elder Neal A. Maxwell made it a practice in his home to hold a family testimony meeting twice a year. He also bore his testimony to his children one on one, wanting his children to know that what he felt and said in private was the same as what they might hear him say over the pulpit.[7] We are promised a cleansing of the spirit when a pure testimony is borne with the Spirit (see D&C 62:3). The Spirit will bear witness of the testimony we share as we do so in a spirit of meekness (see D&C 100:5–8).

- **Access the Savior's gift of repentance daily**. Studying about the priceless gift of the Atonement is essential, but using its cleansing, comforting, and enabling power is just as important. We are told by Alma that procrastination to repent will allow the devil "power over" us (Alma 34:35). Alma also reminded us that we should "acknowledge [our] unworthiness before God at all times" (Alma 38:14). Repentance requires a confessing and forsaking of our sins (see D&C 58:42–43), as well as a change of heart (see Alma 36:6–24), so the Savior's loving mercy can be our companion and the demands of justice can be properly appeased (see Alma 42:15–30). If we will continue to repent and seek to worthily partake of the sacrament each week, then we are promised continued progress toward becoming like Christ (see D&C 20:77–79 and 3 Nephi 18:28–29).

{ Conclusion }

Nephi's powerful words in the Book of Mormon suggest that as a father, husband, and prophet, he had paid the price to come to know the Savior and made every effort to point his family toward Christ. He stated,

> And we talk of Christ, we rejoice in Christ, we preach of Christ, we prophesy of Christ, and we write according to our prophecies, that our children may know to what source they may look for a remission of their sins. (2 Nephi 25:26)

Elder Russell M. Nelson once said,

> As we go through life, even through very rough waters, a father's instinctive impulse to cling tightly to his wife or to his children may not be the best way to accomplish his objective. Instead, if he will lovingly cling to the Savior and the iron rod of the gospel, his family will want to cling to him and to the Savior.
>
> This lesson is surely not limited to fathers. Regardless of gender, marital status, or age, individuals can choose to link themselves directly to the Savior, hold fast to the rod of His truth, and lead by the light of that truth. By so doing, they become examples of righteousness to whom others will want to cling.[8]

It is my hope that each of us can see the great significance of linking ourselves to the Savior and help our families do the same. I conclude with my own personal witness that I know, by the power of the Spirit, that Jesus Christ is our Savior and Redeemer and that His way is the only way to truly find peace and happiness in this life, and ultimately eternal life with our Father in Heaven. I'm grateful for the moments I have walked in His shadow and been a recipient of His marvelous light and inexpressible love, knowing at those times that He has been near indeed. How patient He has been with me as I have sought to do His will, often falling short before being forgiven, cleansed, and trusted once more. I give honor and glory to His name and continue to pledge myself to His service. I know His way is the only way. I hope I might one day prove myself worthy of His sacrifice and be among the "just men made perfect through Jesus the mediator of the new covenant, who wrought out this perfect atonement through the shedding of his own blood" (D&C 76:69).

{ Notes }

1. Henry B. Eyring, "Our Hearts Knit as One," *Ensign*, November 2008.

2. See *Teachings of Presidents of the Church: Joseph Smith* (Salt Lake City: The Church of Jesus Christ of Latter-day Saints, 2007), 49–50.

3. Tad R. Callister, *The Infinite Atonement* (Salt Lake City: Deseret Book, 2000), 2.

4. Richard G. Scott, "Temple Worship: The Source of Strength and Power in Times of Need," *Ensign*, May 2009.

5. Quoted in Boyd K. Packer, "President Spencer W. Kimball: No Ordinary Man," *Ensign*, March 1974, 4.

6. Boyd K. Packer, "The Candle of the Lord," *Ensign*, January 1983.

7. See Bruce C. Hafen and Neal A. Maxwell, *A Disciple's Life* (Salt Lake City: Deseret Book, 2002), 232.

8. Russell M. Nelson, " 'Set in Order Thy House,' " *Ensign*, November 2001, 69.

A Child's Tribute

Just recently, I watched a young man enter the mission field. He helped baptize several of his friends before ever submitting his papers to serve a full-time mission. I had taught him in the ninth grade and watched him mature over the years. He went from someone who had a somewhat dark and difficult past to someone full of goodness and light because of his changed heart and decision to follow Christ. I had fully expected him to be called on a mission back to his native land of Argentina or thereabouts. I was quite surprised when the call finally came for him to serve in the Idaho Boise Mission. He was ecstatic about the call to say the least. He pledged himself with great excitement and anticipation toward serving with all his heart for two years among a people he knew and fully expected to come to love and appreciate. He is one of the many examples of the youth I have met over the years who love the Lord and desire to do His will by going where He wants them go, saying what He wants them to say, doing what He wants them to do, and being what He wants them to be.[1] Elder Neal A. Maxwell was once heard to say, "The youth of this generation have a greater capacity for obedience than any previous generation."[2] The evidence of the truthfulness of this statement seems to be everywhere! How blessed we should feel for the opportunity to parent at such a time when our examples and teachings as parents are more likely to be remembered and internalized. Because of this, it is imperative that we do the best we can to put everything we have to offer on the altar, with the hopes, desire, and faith that the Lord will magnify our efforts and reward us accordingly.

A few years ago, I received one of these so-called rewards quite unexpectedly. I had been invited to attend a Primary event where we were to engage in a type of game show with our daughters. Each girl and her father were asked questions quietly and separately about the other to see if their answers matched. The questions included things such as likes, dislikes, and interests. If the answers matched, the father's tie was to stay intact. However, if the answers were not similar, the father's tie was to be partially snipped off with a pair of scissors. The father and daughter with the longest tie were designated the winner of the event. I was grateful the Primary presidency had decided to bring a collection of old, hideous ties for us dads to use, because all of our ties had been snipped more than once before the game finally concluded. I quickly realized how hard it was to try to come up with what we thought our children would say we would say, for instance, about our favorite food or our favorite vacation spot. For the last and final question, a member of the Primary presidency pulled out her paper and read, "What would your child say you like to do with your free time?" I sat there for a moment before I realized what was really being asked. My chair seemed to feel a little warmer than it had before. I noticed that the question—at first glance appearing harmless—seemed to also make the other dads a little uncomfortable. As I sat there, I thought of the possible answers that might follow, such as "My dad comes home and watches television all night," or "My dad spends countless hours on his laptop away from us." You might pause and ask yourself how your own children would answer such a question. I did, and I'll admit it was a little painful doing so because I knew as a father I had often fallen short of what was expected of me or simply not done my best. In fact, there were days I'm sure Heavenly Father was more than disappointed in me.

I don't remember my guess at what she would say for this last question, but I do remember her response as if it were yesterday: "My dad likes to play and be with me when he has free time. We play basketball together in the driveway." Her simple words echoed in my ears, melted my heart, and filled me with an unexpected and inexpressible joy. I knew the Lord was pleased with my efforts as a father despite the fact that I was far from perfect. There was no special fanfare, no crowds cheering their approval, and no special award or recognition from the Primary presidency for such an answer. There was just a quiet self-assurance that I was loved and that seeking to make my family a priority was and would continue to be the greatest and most rewarding work I would ever be engaged in. I believe that small parental moments such as these—"parental joy" moments, I would call them—occur on occasion to point us toward making commitments to do better in our efforts to love and lift, strengthen and lead. They help us set and reset our priorities toward those things that matter most. I have found that nothing can quite compare to the quiet and sublime feeling that can come from a loving Father in Heaven when your sacrifices as a parent have been acceptable to Him, and when your children are found walking on the path that leads to His presence and all He has to offer. I have found that this joy is unique and remarkable and requires time, energy, and great effort to obtain. May we all consistently seek more knowledge and understanding from above regarding this, the most important work we will do here on the earth. It will be worth all the time, energy, and effort we give toward improving ourselves as parents, and we will find "no greater joy" than it (3 John 1:4).

{ Notes }

1. See "I'll Go Where You Want Me to Go," *Hymns*, no. 270.
2. Neal A. Maxwell, quoted in David A. Bednar, "Heartfelt and Willing Obedience," BYU–Idaho Campus Education Week Devotional, June 27, 2002.

About the Author

Darren E. Schmidt was raised in Layton, Utah, and was one of six children. He served a mission for The Church of Jesus Christ of Latter-day Saints in Wellington, New Zealand. He attended the University of Utah and received a bachelor's degree in psychology as well as a master's degree in educational psychology in 2006. He and his wife and sweetheart, Jolynn, are the parents of eight children (five boys and three girls) and reside in West Jordan, Utah.

Darren has been teaching seminary and institute in Salt Lake City for the seminaries and institutes of religion for more than fifteen years. He is a regular speaker at BYU Education Week, teaching both youth and adult classes, as well as a speaker and session director for Especially for Youth programs. An avid sports fan, Darren loves coaching youth sports teams and running sports clinics for children and youth through evening community education programs. He also loves music, video editing, good humor, singing with his wife and children, and spending time with his family.